Destination: Inspiration!

*Charting Your Course in a
Turbulent World*

PAUL SCHNABEL

ISBN: 978-1-64184-393-5 (Paperback)
ISBN: 978-1-64184-394-2 (Ebook)

With special gratitude to Jody, the best, most supportive wife a guy could have. I'm so glad you're my traveling partner in this life.

And to Austin, who has been a treasured gift since the beginning. I've always got your back.

CONTENTS

ACKNOWLEDGEMENTS

The process of writing this book, which took several years of effort and many years of experiences, led me to feelings of immeasurable gratitude for the people that I've had the privilege of working with and learning from over these past decades.

First, I'd like to thank my friends and colleagues from the Advantage Performance Group and The Real Learning Company, for the opportunities to do great work while having tremendous fun over the years. Your thinking and ideas have helped me to ideate, shape and test many of the concepts contained in this book.

Specifically, I'd like to thank Richard Hodge and Jon Hodge, for their unwavering belief in my capabilities and expert guidance, support and friendship over the years. The opportunities they have afforded me to work with amazing clients while delivering world class learning solutions provided an education no graduate school could emulate.

I'd also like to thank John Hoskins, who took a chance on me years ago and through his example and encouragement inspired me to not just write but publish my own book. John is always ready to listen and never fails to deliver solid advice.

This book wouldn't have been possible without all the awesome clients and participants in my workshops and seminars over the years. Your support, willingness to listen and try out new behaviors and skills, and report back on your accomplishments provided the epiphany I needed to get these concepts into a book.

I couldn't have accomplished this undertaking without the unconditional love and support of my family, who have patiently listened to my ideas, gave me feedback and supported me when self-doubt clouded my thinking. "Thank you" doesn't come close to encompassing the immense gratitude and love that I feel for you.

Lastly, I'd like to thank my Mom, Helen, who is watching all of this from Heaven. She was the first person to believe in my writing abilities, who saved everything I'd ever written in a scrapbook, and to whom I can finally say, "Look Mom, we did it!" Love you always.

INTRODUCTION

We live and work in challenging times. M. Scott Peck opened his blockbuster book, *The Road Less Traveled,* with the simple yet profound statement, "Life is difficult." If you think things are easy, perhaps you're not paying attention. If the Covid-19 virus didn't drive that point home, nothing will.

Spend just a few minutes browsing social media, watching TV, or talking to friends or colleagues; what quickly becomes crystal clear is that we live within a complicated, confusing, often overwhelming jumble of opinions, dogma, and expectations. Our work worlds are not that different; some organizations I've worked with have adopted the military acronym VUCA to describe the changing and challenging environment they operate in: Volatile, Uncertain, Complex, and Ambiguous. I would take it one step further and say that the pandemic has taken VUCA and put it on steroids. The pace and scale of change are breathtaking. One leader I worked with recently said, "It feels like I'm trying to change a tire on a moving car."

This feeling of being pulled in a bazillion different directions, trying to multitask (a proven fallacy), do it all, be good at it all, and enjoy ourselves in the process isn't sustainable. Eventually, our internal temperatures go from a slow simmer to a boil, and we experience various degrees of frustration, burnout, overwhelm, and exasperation. It's really hard to live to good purpose under these conditions. It's really hard to feel contented and satisfied at work and home when you feel like your time is not your own. It's hard to live an inspired life under these circumstances.

The World Needs Inspired People

Inspired people stand out in a crowd. They stand out at work. They show up differently than others because they have a spark, a passion, a desire to make their workplace better, to be a leader in their families, to laugh easily, and lift others. In other words, they are engaged. Companies spend lots of time and money trying to measure and improve employee engagement; it's one of the hot topics in organizational development today.

When I think of an engaged employee or individual, they go beyond mere compliance with their job requirements—they bring true commitment to what they do. A merely compliant employee says, in essence, "Okay boss, you need me to give you THIS MUCH, well guess what? That's all you'll get." On the other hand, a truly committed employee says, "I'm going to take it one, two, three steps further. I'm going to look for ways to improve the work. I'm going to try to make the team better. I'm going to work hard at creating new value for our customers." An engaged employee invests discretionary effort, which is well above the bare minimum required to keep a job and close to the maximum effort one can exert. Engaged people are inspired and serve to inspire others both through words and actions. Their inspiration is authentic because you can't fake inspiration. However, many of us try to do just that. I know, because I tried to do that for a long time.

My Epiphany

I grew up in the Boston area and spent the early part of my career in a variety of sales and sales leadership positions. While I was successful at the work I did and outwardly appeared to be happy and inspired, I was far from it on the inside. What started as a barely detectable feeling that I should be doing something else with my life became a force that was too big to ignore. I knew that I needed to make a shift in my career, but wasn't sure how to do it or what it would look like. After all, I had recently become a dad, and my wife transitioned to full-time motherhood, so I was the primary breadwinner in the household. It certainly wasn't a time to be throwing caution to the wind and making a major career transition. I tried to dismiss my feelings and just keep my head down and work harder, but I started having bouts of depression and anxiety. There were days I said to myself, "How much longer do I have to do this?"

Then, as fate would have it, several events occurred, which took my life in a very different direction.

The first of these events was a car accident I was involved in, just a few minutes from my house when I was out running errands. I was stopped behind another driver making a left-hand turn when someone behind me, who wasn't paying attention, drove right into the back of my car and pushed me into the car in front of me. My car was smaller than either of the cars between me, so I got sandwiched pretty good and ended up with a concussion and a torn labrum in my shoulder. My car was a total loss, but it could have been a lot worse. The silver lining in this incident for me was that it made me realize that all we have is today, that there is no promise of tomorrow. Tomorrow may never come. So, putting my life on hold, or "sucking it up," seemed like a less viable option than it previously had.

The second event was the recognition that my Texan wife, Jody, had never really adjusted to life in New England (something about the long cold winters, I suppose) and was eager to move to a sunnier, warmer climate. It might have been when she said, "You know, I don't see myself getting old here," that I had a moment of clarity! I had never considered a relocation from the area I loved, but valued staying married more and agreed to start the process of looking for a new area to call home.

The third and final event involved my company at the time, which had just merged with two other companies. If you've been through a merger of two companies, you know how difficult it can be; three companies merging is like planets colliding.

Our CEO at the time asked me to take charge of planning our first-ever all-hands meeting, involving over 800 people. Being the ever-dutiful employee, I agreed to do it, but stewed about it all the way home and vociferously complained to Jody that night at dinner. "I can't believe I have to do this. I've never done anything like this before!" Always full of wisdom, my wife suggested I give it a shot and that who knows, maybe I would end up enjoying it.

Well, once I dug into the work, I found that I really did enjoy it. I loved building out the agenda, scheduling the general and breakout sessions, arranging for speakers and presenters. I was also excited about what the conference might represent in terms of a new beginning for our newly combined company. Although the merger had only been completed several months ago, there had been a lot of infighting, power struggles, and confusion over who did what and how they should do it. I viewed this conference as a chance to make a fresh start.

The conference was scheduled for July that year and was to be held in Scottsdale, Arizona. Why Scottsdale in July, you may ask? It was cheap! Our thinking was, *Hey, so what if it's hot? We're going to be in meetings all day, so what does it matter?*

When I arrived in Scottsdale, I was hoping for the best but prepared for the worst. Would everything go according to plan? Would the conference serve to pull us together, get us aligned behind a common vision, and set us on a strong path for the future? All of these thoughts were running through my mind when I stood on the podium in front of all 800 employees as the conference co-host to kick off the four-day meeting.

Energy-wise, things started off a little slowly, with people not knowing everybody there and tending to stick to their cliques. However, slowly but surely, people's defenses started to break down—they started to get to know each other as real people, not just a voice on the telephone or a name sending an email. The best bonding happened evenings in the gigantic hotel pool, where relationships were strengthened, and people loosened up and started having fun. I started to feel like we had turned an important corner in our evolution as a company.

On the third day, we hired a motivational speaker named Keith Harrell, who fired up the group and delivered a powerful message about taking control of your destiny. I took the message to heart and started thinking about my own destiny that night in my hotel room. Initially, I had come to enjoy conference organizing but, more importantly, had really enjoyed and felt comfortable in my role as emcee. I had never spoken in front of 800 people prior to the conference but found that I was pretty good at it, and thought about how I might take my career in a different direction.

Due to Keith's message and my awe and wonder at watching people come together over the course of the event, I decided to take a risk. The next day was the fourth and final day of our conference, and I was supposed to take a few minutes at the start of the day to go over the day's agenda and introduce the first speaker. Instead, I stayed up all night in my hotel room to write a speech I would deliver where I shared my excitement for what I had been doing these past four days and my hope for us as a company going forward. I wondered how the CEO would react; after all, isn't the head honcho supposed to deliver that kind of rousing message? But I decided to act first and seek forgiveness later, also thinking that such a message might have more credibility and impact coming from me, as a peer to most of the people in the room.

When my time came to speak, as people were just settling in with their coffee and notebooks, I had prearranged for the AV technicians to drop the lights and play some loud, upbeat music as I walked on the stage. That got the crowd's attention! Then I proceeded to deliver the message I had prepared, speaking from the heart and ending with a call for us to take this momentum back to our jobs and make this company great.

The audience stood and gave me a standing ovation as I left the stage, and at that moment, I had what I can only call an epiphany—a true moment of inspiration—that this is what I needed to do with my life! It was a way in which I could take all my collective work experience and bring it to people in a new way.

I not only resolved to start a speaking and training practice but decided that Arizona would be the place to do it from. Despite the July heat, I fell in love with the desert and thought I'd absolutely adore it in January! I flew home, shared my epiphany with Jody, and she said, "Well, I've never been there, but it sounds good, so let's go!" Four months later, we'd sold the house, and my wife, our four-year-old son, and I moved to Scottsdale, leaving family and friends behind and not knowing one person in our new area.

That happened over twenty years ago, and we're still here. I share this story because the last twenty years have been the best, the most inspired years of my life. Speaking, training, and coaching others is the work I love to do, and I couldn't imagine what my life would have been like if fate hadn't intervened as it did all those years ago. I no longer ask myself, "How long do I HAVE to do this?" Instead, I ask, "How long do I GET to do this?"

Destination Inspiration—With a Twist

What I've described is not just inspiration but *practical* inspiration. I use this term because inspiration should produce more than good feelings that don't translate into actions and benefits for others. Practical inspiration means that not only do you benefit, but so do your coworkers, your family, your friends, and your community. We have seen countless examples of inspiration in action during the COVID-19 pandemic as multitudes of people stepped up to effect positive change, whether it was bagging groceries, supporting societal change, or using their talents to lift the spirits of others. None of it is about sitting on the mountaintop and waiting for inspiration to hit you like a bolt out of the clear blue sky. If that happens to you, great! You may hope that it does. But hope alone makes for a lousy strategy. What it's about is the willingness to create the conditions and establish the habits required to become practically inspired.

Some of you may be thinking, *There's no way I can make that type of shift. It's just not practical.* I would suggest it's not only practical but possible. It first begins with a recognition that you want things to be different for you. That you would like to be more inspired and effective at your job, at home, and in your community. That perhaps, just perhaps, the things you have been doing are no longer working for you, and that it's time to think differently and do differently. As they used to say in the Old West, it's time to stop riding that dead horse.

When your horse dies, dismount!

The next step is to be open to changing things up. I'm not suggesting everyone needs to make radical changes in their careers or location as I did, but can you make small, practical changes in mindset and behavior that lead to practical, long-lasting inspiration that lifts up those you come in contact with? Are you ready to learn and grow? For being a learner is a hallmark of an inspired life, and is especially critical in a fast-changing, VUCA world. Educator Eric Hoffer said it best when he wrote, "During times of change, the *learners* will inherit the earth, while the *learned* are perfectly equipped to deal with a world that no longer exists."

What I've Learned

I've spent the last twenty years of my career working with a wide variety of people to develop the skills required for lasting success. I've worked with over 40,000 frontline leaders and executives, salespeople and engineers, customer service reps and doctors. I've had the opportunity to consult with and understand the challenges of working in a variety of organizations, including large Fortune 100 companies, small startups, healthcare organizations, and nonprofits. I've traveled through North America, Europe, Central America, and Asia to help leaders lead, sellers sell, and individuals thrive. The opportunity to do this work has been an amazing gift and blessing, and I have enjoyed every minute of it!

Through these personal experiences, observations, and research, I've learned a few things along the way that are central to this book. First is that I've had the opportunity to observe and learn from people who are the epitome of living an inspired life. By trying to understand what they do differently from others to create sustained inspiration, and through trial and error in my own life, I've captured some key principles that will form the central part of this book.

Secondly, I've learned that by identifying and focusing our efforts on a discreet number of high impact tasks and behaviors, we can develop and grow exponentially. It's like when I took my first golf lesson. I was coached to focus on a number of things as I addressed the ball and initiated my swing sequence, including keeping my head down, keeping my head still, making sure my left heel is on the ground, sweeping the club back low and straight, turning my hips in conjunction with my backswing, pausing at the top of my backswing, following through high after impact, and keeping my eye on the ball. I was thinking so much and was so confused that my game got ten strokes *worse* after my lessons, not better! I finally stopped the lessons and focused on just one of those things. By doing that, my game improved, and once that practice became a habit, I then focused on the next thing.

This is one of the challenges that people face when they finish any kind of learning or training experience. If the training has struck a chord, they may have ten, fifteen, or twenty things they want to learn and apply. These might include things they want to start doing or things they need to stop doing, or maybe do differently. The problem, like my golf lesson example, is that it is virtually impossible to change that many things at once, so guess what happens? People quickly get discouraged because by trying to do too many things, by trying to "boil the ocean," they end up mastering nothing and soon quit trying.

Therefore, the first principle in this book is to identify and implement the actions that will create a high impact and be relatively simple to implement as a starting point. Referring to the 2x2 matrix that follows, we will focus our energies in the top left quadrant.

Impact

	High	**Low**
Easy	Focus Here	
Difficult		

Ease of Implementing

Once you have exhausted all possibilities for growth in the top left quadrant, then you can consider actions that fall into the difficult but high impact category. By that point, you'll have the momentum you've created to tackle those areas that will reap additional rewards for you.

A Path to Fulfillment Through the Seven Cs

Identifying high impact actions to set your destination to practical inspiration is the foundation of this effort. I liken the journey to setting sail across a shining sea to a brighter future—a future full of passion, purpose, and adventure. Just as there are seven seas on planet Earth, there are seven elements I've put forth here, each beginning with the letter C. They build on each previous element, and each has a particular purpose and area of focus:

Calling: What purpose is calling you in your life, and how are you aligned and behaving with that calling in your everyday work? If there is a gap between your calling and your current circumstances, how can you close that gap? If you don't have a calling, how can you discover or uncover it?

Character: What kind of person are you? What values are important in your life, and are you living in a way that is consistent with them? How are you using the power of habits to establish powerful new behaviors and actions that are aligned with your calling?

Capability: What are you doing to develop and acquire the knowledge and skills that support your calling and are required for lasting success and inspiration? Do you have people in your life who you can learn from and who support your success? Are you sharing what you've learned with others?

Curiosity: Are you interested in learning about and from other people? Do you gladly try to master new things? Are you willing to examine your beliefs or old ideas to see if they are still valid for you? Do you challenge your assumptions and help others to challenge theirs?

Connection: Do you put a value on being fully present with others, demonstrating active listening, and being authentic? Do people walk away from an interaction with you feeling better than before they spoke to you? Do others see you as a leader, regardless of your title?

Centeredness: Are you able to stay grounded and maintain a firm center in the face of stressful situations? Is achieving balance in your life something you believe in and strive for, or have you given up on that idea as unrealistic? Do you bring calm to chaos, or do you contribute to it?

Commitment: Are you able to turn your ideas into sustained action? Do you get easily discouraged when taking on new behaviors if you don't see immediate results, or do you stay the course and keep the momentum going, even if in small increments? Would others say you are steadfast during tough times?

This book can be read front to back, or you can jump in and begin work at any "C" that would create the greatest impact for you at this time. At the end of each chapter, there will be some practical, tangible actions you can use to put these ideas into practice.

You Are Worth It!

Perhaps you are reading this book because you believe you can have a greater impact on others that you work with, and can have a more satisfying career. Maybe the recent pandemic gave you the wake-up call you needed to recognize that you've been stagnant for a while, and the time is right to focus on your personal growth. Maybe it's because you realized that you haven't been truly inspired for a long time and believe you can do better. Whatever reason you have for embarking on a path of personal or professional development, rest assured that you are worth it! You're worth every bit of the investment you make in becoming practically inspired because as you grow and thrive, you have a greater impact on the people you work with, the customers you serve, the families and friends you share your life with. Inspiration is contagious, and there's no benefit to the world by you staying small. As Grant Cardone wrote, "Thinking big takes the same amount of effort as thinking small." Failing to take action means you'll have to live with some level of disappointment or regret, which is hardly the formula for inspired living.

Soon after I moved to Arizona, I was given an opportunity to interview Dr. Elizabeth Kubler-Ross. You may remember her as the developer behind the five stages of grief (denial, anger, bargaining, depression, and acceptance) and as one of the early champions of the hospice movement.

The woman who arranged the interview warned me that Dr. Ross could be a bit challenging. At that time, she was in her early eighties, had suffered multiple strokes, and still smoked cigarettes like a chimney. She told me that if Dr. Ross didn't like me within the first five minutes, she would throw me out of her house. *No pressure there*, I thought.

On the day of the interview, I drove to Dr. Ross's home in North Scottsdale, in the middle of the Sonoran Desert. When I knocked, she called for me to let myself in, and when I entered, I saw her lying on her sofa, smoking a cigarette. She beckoned for me to have a seat, and we began to talk.

After about five minutes, she asked me, "Would you like a cup of tea?" I shook my head slowly and said, "Oh, no thank you, ma'am," to which she replied tersely, "Well I'd like one, so why don't you go ahead and make it for me!" As I walked to the kitchen, I thought to myself, *Well, at least she didn't throw me out!*

We discussed many topics that afternoon, but the one thing that stood out for me was a comment she made about working with the dying. She said, "I've worked with thousands of dying patients over the years, and they often have regrets. But usually, they don't regret things they did, *they regret the things they didn't do.*" Life is too short to live with regret, to not do the things you need to do to become the person you can be. To be a person whose destination is inspiration.

Why wait any longer? The world needs your best, inspired you!

CHAPTER 1

The First C: Calling
What are you waiting for?

Recently, I was having a coaching conversation with a fairly new manager at the request of their leader. This person was promoted into management about a year ago after a very successful stint as an individual contributor. However, it was obvious that he was struggling with his new role. He had not embraced his role as a leader. Instead, he had continued with the mindset and behaviors of an individual contributor, seemingly getting more satisfaction from those activities than his new job requirements to get work done through others.

When his leader talked to him about this, he admitted there was some truth to that, but that he wanted to succeed in his new role. That's where I came in.

After taking some time to establish the relationship, I began asking him some questions about his work history, specifically about his nonmanagement role prior to his promotion, which involved a direct sales role. "Oh, I loved the work," he gushed. "I couldn't wait to get to work in the morning because I really enjoyed being able to meet with customers, solve their problems, and feel like I accomplished something by the end of the day."

Next, I asked how he felt about his new management role. At first, he indicated that he liked it all right, but then he began to open up. "It's frustrating because it seems like all I do is deal with people issues all day. Stuff like needing me to deal with our contracts group, having problems working with others on the team, personal issues that were interfering with their work responsibilities."

When I pointed out that the things he was having issues with were precisely the kinds of things that managers deal with, it was if a light bulb turned on above his head. He realized that he just didn't have the passion for this type of work, that he had taken the offer of a promotion because it involved more prestige and seemed like the thing to do at that point in his career. He realized that his true calling was to be in a nonmanagement selling role.

Fortunately for him and his company, we were able to transition him back into a direct selling role, instead of losing someone who had the talent and track record to succeed, just not in the new role he had been given. The missing piece for him was that he didn't see management as being aligned with his calling, which was to solve customer problems through the services he provided. Back in his old role, he quickly regained his inspiration and was even more successful than he had been previously.

What Is a Calling?

Do a Google search for "calling," and the following definition appears: "A strong urge toward a particular way of life or career; a vocation." If you know someone who is pursuing a calling in life, they are typically pretty inspired people who model any number of admirable human qualities: Focus, agility, determination, and resilience.

Calling is a powerful, more inspired version of purpose; it imbues our thoughts and actions with an energy and spirit that allows people to accomplish great things, or little things greatly. I think about the story of the medieval stone chippers who were constructing a grand cathedral in Europe. A monk was walking through the building area, and when he came across the first stone chipper, asked him what he was doing. "Breaking rocks, what does it look like I'm doing?" replied the first stone chipper brusquely.

The monk moved along quickly and soon came upon a second stone chipper, engaged in a similar task. He also asked this stone chipper what he was doing. His answer, however, was very different than the first stone chipper. "Well, I am building a magnificent cathedral!" That simple illustration highlights the differences between someone who sees their work as drudgery to be endured and someone who sees it as aligned with their calling in life.

I like to go hiking in the mountains of New England when I go back to visit friends and family, and the worst part of the hike for me is always the part where I'm below the treeline, where I can't see my ultimate goal, which is the summit. Once I emerge from the trees and can see the apex of my hike, I get a new spring in my step and more energy for the journey (well, not as much energy as I got when I was in my twenties, but you get the picture).

Staying inspired while we engage in difficult, tedious, or onerous tasks is near impossible without the perspective that having a true purpose—a calling—brings.

"When you dance, your purpose is not to get to a certain place on the floor. It's to enjoy each step along the way."
— Dr. Wayne Dyer

Calling Gives Meaning to Our Efforts

Soon after I turned thirty, and with a desire to push my limits, I participated in an experiential wilderness education program run by Outward Bound. This 28-day multi-element course took place in the backwoods and waters of Maine. It involved a wide range of physical and mental tests, including hiking and orienteering, canoeing and running rapids, sailing and rappelling, taking mentally challenged kids camping, and several other difficult activities. Their motto is "To serve, to strive, and not to yield."

There were eight of us in the group, and two instructors led us. Our lead instructor, Tony, was a swashbuckling, no-nonsense Brit who led Outward Bound trips in the summer, sea kayaked the coast of Alaska on occasion, and gave ski lessons in Switzerland in the winter. Each morning, we would rise around 4:00 am and receive our plans for the day. If we were traveling to another destination, Tony would show us on the map where we were and where we needed to get to. Each day had a very clear purpose—we needed to get from Point A to Point B—and the entire day was spent in that pursuit. First, we would organize ourselves into roles to accomplish our purpose: Navigator, Cook, Team Leader, etc. We would all take ownership of our roles for the day and focus on doing them as best as we could, in order to accomplish our collective purpose and to avoid letting the other team members down.

This was more or less the rhythm of our lives for 28 straight days. Whether it was bushwhacking through the primeval forest, shooting the rapids, or sailing through a thick fog, each day had a very clear purpose that we worked to execute, regardless of fatigue or sickness. We developed strong bonds as a team, due in large part to our coming together to fulfill our given purpose despite significant challenges and obstacles along the way.

One of the key lessons we learned during that experience was that we were able to do more than we previously believed we were capable of. For some, it was the difficult physical challenges; for others, it was the mental challenges we were put through. But in every instance, we found a strength within we didn't know we had, and I came to realize that most of our limitations are self-imposed.

That realization did several things for me. First, it caused me to embrace a bigger version of myself, a self that was capable of achieving more than I thought possible. Second, what helped us as a team achieve greatly was our clear sense of purpose and calling during the journey. Our purpose was to attain each day's milestones. Our calling was to do so by acting as a team, by leaving no person behind, and by being a part of something bigger than each of us as individuals. Each day we had very clear goals and objectives that helped us focus our energies and to lift each other up. "Come on team, only three more miles of paddling to go, and we can set up camp for the night!" We were aligned as a group behind a common calling. Despite our exhaustion, frustration, and weariness at the constant grind and struggle, we were sad to see it end. We all felt this journey was one of our peak life experiences.

What Is Calling You?

Some people are fortunate to have figured out their calling from a very young age. Several years ago, I was watching a program about upcoming Olympic athletes, and I was struck by how many of them indicated that not just being in the Olympics but winning a gold medal had been on their radar since a very young age—in some cases as young as five or seven years old.

I also have several friends whose college-age children discovered their calling during their mid-to-late teens and are now happily pursuing a degree in a discipline they have felt called to for a while, whether that discipline was engineering, accounting, or nursing. Their parents say that having a clear calling or purpose has helped their children stay focused and avoid some of the pitfalls that are all too prevalent for high school or college-age young people.

For others, it is more difficult to develop a calling—that difficulty only increases as they feel the pressure of *not having a calling*. But for most people, it involves a long process of trial and error and saying yes to a wide variety of opportunities, which allows them to go through a process of elimination to figure out what they *don't* want to do, as a prerequisite to discovering what they *do* want to do.

In some cases, it can take years before one's true calling is discerned and followed.

That was how it happened in my case; I spent the first fifteen or so years of my working life being successful but unfulfilled, always feeling like there had to be something more to a career. However, when I finally discovered my true calling, I realized that I needed to go through each and every bit of the previous fifteen years to gain the experience and knowledge that allowed me to pursue my calling with passion and purpose. After all, it's difficult to speak credibly about leadership or sales without having been a leader or salesperson yourself! So, I was able to reframe my early career not as wasted time, but as time invested in enabling my future. My early career years became the cornerstone of my new life's calling.

However, most experts agree that discovering your life's calling needs to be an active process, not a passive one. Sitting on the mountaintop (literally or figuratively) waiting for your calling to tap you on the shoulder may work for an enlightened few but isn't a successful recipe for most of us. Taking purposeful action, coupled with active reflection and discovery, will help almost anyone find their calling.

Reinvention or Reframing?

It is important to note that developing a calling doesn't always require a radical change in your work. In many cases, it might simply involve a change in how you perceive your current work, and how you can be true to your calling through the circumstances you are currently in. Like the stone chipper story I shared earlier, changing how you view your work can often be incredibly liberating and transformative.

For example, I work with many people in the healthcare industry who want to help others but aren't involved in the clinical or patient care side of the work. Can a quality manager, a maintenance worker, or an appointment scheduler reframe what they do so they can see their work being aligned if their calling is to help others? You bet! For without the services of these dedicated folks, many of the operations that deal directly with helping patients would cease to function, or wouldn't function effectively. Creating a line of sight between the work you do and how it connects to your ultimate calling can transform your work into something closer to delight than drudgery.

I read a story several years ago about a janitor in an old-line company that printed checks. It seems the company was taking a new strategic direction in the face of competitive threats, and one of their new commitments was to turn around customer orders within two hours of receipt.

Around this time, two reporters were gathering a story about the company who were taking a tour of the facility during the late-night shift, when they noticed a janitor meticulously cleaning one of the printing machines. They were so struck by the care with which he engaged in his tasks that they just stood there for a few minutes, unnoticed, to watch him work.

Finally, before moving on, one of the reporters tapped the janitor on the shoulder to congratulate him on his attention to detail. Without missing a beat, and without knowing who these people were, the janitor proudly replied, "Well, we have a new pledge to turn around customer orders within two hours. So, if one of these machines is down because it's dirty or not well maintained, we might not be able to keep our commitment to our customers."

When I heard this story I thought, *The janitor gets it!* The janitor, not a role one typically associates with being the champion for a corporate strategy, understood how the work he did was vital to the commitment his company was making. Clearly, this janitor had found his inspiration by connecting the work he did to something greater than his self-interest—a higher calling, if you will. Try hitching your wagon to a bigger purpose, and you might have just discovered your calling.

"If you find what you do each day seems to have no link to any higher purpose, you probably want to rethink what you're doing."
— Ronald A. Heifetz

Are You Your Own Worst Enemy?

I've met many people in my years of speaking and facilitating workshops, and many people who are dissatisfied in their work lives have a very clear calling—they just aren't following it! For a myriad of reasons, they don't believe that they can successfully make a transition in their lives.

In some cases, it's financial. People with families to support or bills to pay often aren't in a position to leave a good-paying job to pursue something that may pay far less, at least initially. My guidance in those cases is to help them find ways to take baby steps in the direction of their calling, whether it's through looking for ways to express their calling in their current work or by spending a few hours a week working toward their desired calling.

But in many other cases, it's a lack of belief in themselves or trust that they can actually manifest the reality they desire. If you feel stuck and think it's due to a lack of skills, knowledge, or opportunities, think again. It may just have something to do with your self-image.

Do you truly value yourself? Until you value yourself, you won't value your time or what you do with it.

Again, do you value yourself? Do you embrace and respect the unique arrangement of talents and motivations that are yours alone and will point you in the direction of your life's calling? Or do you belittle yourself with a negative barrage of self-talk, constantly comparing yourself to others and coming up short?

One thing is certain: You cannot outperform your self-image for long.

Let me repeat that one more time, with feeling: YOU CANNOT OUTPERFORM YOUR SELF-IMAGE FOR LONG. Simply stated, if you find yourself temporarily enjoying a new level of success but believe in your heart you don't deserve it, or that you'll soon be unmasked for the poseur you truly are, then those beliefs will eventually create that reality, and your limiting self-image will be reinforced. Each time we allow ourselves to be derailed in this way makes it more difficult to break this cycle. I hate to sound cliched, *but you gotta believe it to achieve it.*

A long time ago, I knew a little boy in first grade who excelled at reading, and was individually tutored by the teacher using a fifth-grade workbook. However, the boy didn't feel comfortable or capable of this level of performance and, as a result, didn't try his best. Soon enough, he was back in the regular reading circle with the rest of his classmates. His limiting beliefs were the main obstacles that were preventing him from fulfilling his true potential.

If any of this has the ring of truth for you, take a deeper look in the mirror to learn if it's a limiting self-image that is holding you back from chasing your calling. Recognizing the problem is the first step in handling it. You can't redecorate your living room in the dark!

> *"So many of us choose our path out of fear disguised as practicality...*
> *You can fail at what you don't want. So, you might as well take a chance on doing what you love."*
> — Jim Carrey

High Impact Actions for Discovering Your Calling

If you aren't clear on what your calling is, here are some actions you can take to gain greater clarity or get unstuck.

Who are you, really?

On the surface, this question may seem to have an easy answer, but don't go so fast. Are you living with other people's conceptions of who you are and what you are capable of, what you are good or not good at? Have you allowed well-intended coworkers, friends, and family to create a tidy little box for you, which you have dutifully climbed right into?

Who are you? Truthfully answering this question requires courage and the willingness to shine a light into the darkened recesses of your mind. A truthful answer to this question requires you to think for yourself, which is not always an easy task and is counter to many of the forces we encounter in the world every day. Following what someone else thinks should be your calling is a recipe for unhappiness.

That is not to say that we shouldn't seek the opinion of those close to us in order to gain a fuller perspective on our strengths and development opportunities, as a vehicle for uncovering our calling. Sometimes we aren't the best judge of our truest selves, especially if we are prone to self-loathing at one extreme or grandiosity at the other. I have found that we are rarely as incapable as we think at our worst, or as perfect as we think at our best. The truth is usually somewhere in the middle, and people who are close to us and have our best interests in mind can often help us see ourselves in the proper light.

⇒ **HIGH IMPACT ACTION:** Pick three people who know you very well and want the best for you. It may be family members, work colleagues, or friends. Talk with each of them separately, and tell them you are seeking their feedback for some important self-development. Ask them what they perceive you to be good at, both in terms of skills (measurable, quantifiable things like computer programming, driving a vehicle, or welding) and competencies (behaviors such as team building, creativity, and problem-solving). Ask them to be as specific as possible. Take notes, then compare their responses. Where are there patterns and commonalities in the feedback? How does their input align with or differ from your ideas?

Connect to your peak experiences

We've all had times in our lives when we were at our absolute best, moments when we were so engaged in what we were doing that the passing of hours felt like minutes. Maybe they were in a work setting, or at home. Maybe it happened a long time ago, perhaps when you were a child, or maybe it just happened recently. In either case, connecting with these peak experiences can provide real insight into your calling.

⇒ **HIGH IMPACT ACTION:** Find a quiet place, close your eyes, and let your mind drift back to a time in your life that was a peak experience for you. Maybe it was a work experience, something at school, or a sport or physical activity. Close your eyes and transport yourself back to that time and place until it becomes very vivid in your mind. What were you feeling and experiencing in those moments?

After several minutes, write down as much as you can about each moment, providing as much detail as possible. Details about what you were feeling and thinking, as well as what you were doing and experiencing. Do this exercise several times for a few days, to make sure you're not leaving out any important experiences. Then, try to see what these peak experiences had in common for you. Was there any overlap between your peak experiences and what you learned in the previous exercise?

Do some research

As you start to gain a clearer sense of direction and purpose, it may be worthwhile to do some research into what it might take to follow your calling. If you've decided that your calling is to become a leader in your current career, what steps will you need to take to get on that path? What skills, knowledge, and tools will you need to develop to set you up for success if and when you've been allowed to step into that role? If your calling requires a change in career direction, can you find people to speak with who are already working in that field, who could share their insights on what it takes to succeed? What education might you need to acquire, and how will you get it?

⇒ **HIGH IMPACT ACTION:** Commit to spending at least two hours per week doing research that will help you move into your calling. Don't just do online research but talk to people who may be helpful and provide insights. Say yes to opportunities that may provide valuable perceptions and experiences. Ask your friends and colleagues if they know of anyone with knowledge in the areas you are pursuing that you should speak with. Sometimes it's not about what people know, but who they know.

Craft your calling declaration

Putting words to your calling and then putting those words to computer or paper is a critical step in breathing life into your efforts. There is power in seeing words on a page, a power that manifests as accountability and focus for your pursuit. This is the first real step in making the intangible tangible!

⇒ **HIGH IMPACT ACTION:** Write down your answers to the following questions. Make it part of your daily routine to look at your declaration and commitments, and if possible, post them in a visible place where you can see them throughout the day. If desired, you can also share your calling with those who are closest to you, but choose who you reveal this to wisely. Avoid negative individuals who may rain on your parade.

<u>My Calling is:</u>
(Be as descriptive as you can while also keeping it simple. For example, "My calling is to help make the world a more beautiful place through the landscaping services that I provide.")

_____

_____

_____

_____

_____

_____

_____

Actions I will take to be true to my calling:
(You can start acting true to your calling right now! Again, be as specific as you can here. For example, "I will learn the skills I need to succeed" isn't as good as "I will learn C++ programming through an online school by December 31st.")

_____
_____
_____
_____
_____
_____
_____
_____

What will I feel and experience when I am living my calling?
(Put yourself into the picture and get specific about the benefits you'll derive from being true to your calling. For example, "I will be excited to get up and go to work each day. I will be grateful for the chance to give back to others through the work that I do.")

_____
_____
_____
_____
_____
_____
_____
_____

What is the downside if I don't follow my calling?
(It's important to recognize the price you will pay by not honoring yourself and your chosen direction. Is the price a feeling that you're not maximizing your potential? Feelings of settling for less? Wasting your talent? Frustration and unhappiness? If you are having trouble identifying the downsides to not following your calling, then you'll be easily

discouraged and more likely to throw in the towel when the going gets tough.)

The One Thing to Remember Even if You Forget Everything Else in This Chapter: DON'T DELAY, BEGIN TODAY!

While research will start to build a solid foundation for the pursuit of your calling, don't get stuck in this phase, or as some say, "analysis paralysis." Do enough research to get the understanding you need, but recognize that you'll never have complete or perfect information about many things in life, and at some point, you just need to make a commitment and go for it.

Clarity of calling and purpose creates power, so just get started! Begin the habit of regular and honest self-appraisal to stay on track. Replace your negative self-talk with empowering messages. Get a good coach or mentor whom you trust, and are willing to be honest with.

It's also important to be patient with yourself. There will be many times along the journey when you may take two steps back for every one step forward. You may feel stuck or discouraged.

If you find yourself in that place, ask, "What are one or two small things I can do today to move toward my calling?" Maybe it's picking up the phone and calling someone who works in the field you're pursuing. If it's a perceived obstacle that is stopping you, think of actions you can take to minimize or mitigate the obstacle. Maybe it's rereading the thoughts you've already put to paper in this chapter.

Taking these actions in one day will get your energy flowing constructively again and will produce a greater sense of control and the personal power required to press on toward your calling.

"Be as you wish to seem."
— Socrates

Remember, it's the little things done consistently that lead to lasting success. Want to read more this year, but can't find the time? Well, can you find ten minutes? If you can read for just ten minutes per day this year and you're an average reader, you should finish around six books. Want to sell more? Make just one extra sales call per day, and you'll talk to approximately 220 more people this year. Robin Sharma wrote, "The smallest of actions is greater than the noblest of intentions." So, keep taking small, consistent actions in the pursuit of your dreams. Don't allow discouragement or inertia to rob you of the opportunity to pursue and live the calling you dream of.

That little boy in first grade you met earlier in this chapter was me, but with persistence and encouragement from family and teachers, I moved past my self-limiting beliefs. Take heart that the only way you can fail is to give up. Stay on course, and you'll be amazed how doors open up to help bring your dreams and your calling into reality!

CHAPTER 2

The Second C: Character
What you do, even when no one is looking, matters

The hardest talk I've ever had to give in my life was a eulogy for one of my best friends, Gary, who left this world at the far too young age of forty-two. Gary was taken in the prime of his life, leaving behind a loving and devoted wife, two young children, and a bevy of friends and relatives.

I had been friends with Gary since high school, and our friendship developed further when we attended the same college together. With a variety of other friends, we would hang out in the cafeteria, tended bar together on the weekends, and took many road trips to celebrate our newfound freedom and to satisfy our wanderlust to explore the world.

Our most unforgettable trip was when Gary, our friend Rich, and I took one summer in between semesters to drive cross-country to see America, camping or sleeping in the car along the way, forging bonds and memories to last a lifetime. The trip was hatched over a cold beer in a dive bar, as we debated whether to work that summer and save money or travel the country instead. We were on the fence about which decision to make at the outset, but by the third beer, the choice was obvious. (Not recommending this as a life planning strategy, but it worked out that time!)

*Selfie of Gary and Paul climbing Mount Washington,
NH, October 2000*

After college, I pursued a career in sales, while Gary leveraged his degree and became an accountant. After several years, he realized that being an accountant was not his life's calling and began a new career search in earnest. Gary was always outgoing, personable, and built relationships effortlessly, so I suggested he might consider a career in sales. As he gave this idea some serious consideration, it so happened that a job opportunity in sales opened up in my company and I let him know about it, while putting in a good word for him with the boss.

Gary was hired for that job and, after a few years of success, found a position with a startup company in the telecommunications industry, with a ground-floor position in direct sales, with most of his time spend cold calling and prospecting for new customers. While many others fell by the wayside, Gary thrived in that environment and through hard work and dedication his career grew as the company grew, to a point where he eventually ended up with the role of Vice President of Sales for a company that now was generating 500 million dollars a year in revenue.

He was in that role when he died, and over 1,000 of his closest family, friends, and coworkers came to pay tribute to Gary at his funeral. Gary's dad, brother, and I all spoke at the service, and afterward, we gathered nearby for a celebration of his life.

While I knew many of the people who were there, there were many people I didn't know and tried to meet as many of them as I could. A number of them were current and former employees who had worked for Gary, with some of them traveling long distances to come to the funeral, while still others had worked for him ten or fifteen years ago and hadn't seen him since. When I asked these people why they took the time or made the sacrifice to come and pay tribute to Gary, the responses were strikingly similar.

"Gary always made time to listen to me."

"Gary gave me tough love when I needed it, telling me things I didn't want to hear but that made a huge difference in my life and career."

"Gary never asked us to do anything he wasn't willing to do himself. He really 'walked the talk' and always did the right thing."

"He had an incredible work ethic, which rubbed off on the rest of us."

"I learned more from Gary in one year of working with him than I've learned in twelve years since."

When I went back to my hotel that day, I reflected on the comments I heard. It made me realize how critically important having impeccable character was to living an inspired life and making an impact on others. It also made me realize that in forty-two short years, Gary was able to leave behind an amazing legacy through the work he did and the people he positively affected on a regular basis. To this day, I use his example to motivate me to give my best even when I don't feel like it, and to live each day to the fullest and in accordance with my values.

Character Starts with Values

Values are those fundamental beliefs that we deem to be important, which can help us navigate life and guide important actions and decisions. So, what do you truly value in life? It's an important question, but one that many of us rarely spend time consciously thinking about. Sure, if asked, we may quickly come up with things like our family, regular exercise, or having close friends, but have we thought about what qualities of character we truly value and wish to embody? For what we *say* we value and what our behavior reveals about what we *actually* value can be two different things.

For example, someone might say that they value openness and honesty, yet find themselves telling "little white lies" to avoid difficult conversations or as a way to cover up for a work project that didn't go as planned. Or, someone may say they value having work/life balance, but model just the opposite to those they live and work with.

Some values are more fleeting and may change with time. When I was in my twenties, I valued the freedom to come and go as I pleased, but when I got married and started a family, I discarded those ideals in exchange for the values of having a stable and secure home and rich family life. As we grow and evolve throughout our lives, some values may take on greater or lesser significance. That's just the natural evolution of things.

It can also be useful to note the distinction between the values that guide us and the things we value. For example, we may value airbags in the cars we drive, but the personal value that having airbags supports is safety.

So what values are important to you? Do you value dependability, courage, or having a sense of humor? What about living from a spiritual center or maintaining a spirit of adventure? What about compassion, achievement, honesty, or trustworthiness? Search for the word "values," and you'll find a far more exhaustive list of possible values you might reflect upon. Think about which ones resonate the strongest with you and why, eventually landing on a smaller set of core values that best summarize who you are and what you aspire to be. For values can be both demonstrable and aspirational at the same time.

For instance, one of my core values is compassion, which I think about often and try to demonstrate with regularity. However, I'm also clear that I can become more compassionate than I currently am, with the understanding that I'll never reach a state of perfection. But having an attitude of continuous improvement and progress in pursuit of living your values is vital.

Excuse Me, But Your Character Is Showing

Having a strong set of values that are more than just words on a piece of paper helps you stay strong and committed to your calling, supports decision-making that aligns with your values, and helps you to do the next right thing, whether in public or in private. To me, that is the epitome of character. What do you do when no one is looking? If we cut corners or rationalize behavior that is misaligned with who we are striving to be, there's a cost, whether you are fully aware of it at that moment or not.

Do you behave well with some people and badly with others? I believe in the adage that a person's character is revealed not by how they treat someone in a position of power but someone that they have power over. Someone who is the model of decency to a CEO but barks at the receptionist or the waiter in the restaurant is strongly revealing their lack of character. I read a Tweet recently by a hiring manager who was on the subway to work one morning to interview a candidate for a job position. While on the train, someone brushed by him rudely while sending a few choice words in his direction. When the hiring manager got to his office, guess who the job candidate was? It's great when karma gets served so instantaneously, but it always gets served eventually.

Difficult circumstances may or may not build character, but they certainly reveal it. People can talk a good game, but how do they behave in the real world? A value without a behavior is merely an opinion.

Remember that those who can be trusted with small things can be trusted with larger things. Become someone that you are proud to look at in the mirror every morning and every night.

How Would Others Describe You?

One of the tools used in business today is the 360-degree feedback assessment. This tool involves polling a variety of colleagues, leaders, and direct reports (if you have any), and asking a multitude of questions about your effectiveness in the role you have. In my experience working in leadership development, this is one of the most powerful tools available to reinforce good behaviors and to call out harmful ones.

It is powerful because we are often blind to many of our behaviors, which spring from our character. Years ago, I learned the Johari Window model, which is a 2x2 matrix as follows:

Johari Window

	Known to self	Not known to self
Known to others	Arena	Blind Spot
Not known to others	Façade	Unknown

We all have some elements of character that show up in the quadrant labeled *Known to others, Not known to self.* These are our blind spots, and it's vital to get feedback in these areas to understand how certain behaviors may be negatively impacting our work colleagues, manager, or customers. Sometimes, just being made aware of these behaviors is enough to change them. I've had many conversations with people I was coaching about things they were doing that negatively impacted others, and often their response was, "Oh my gosh, I had no idea this is what people were feeling." In other cases, coaching, mentoring, or skill development can be effective in addressing "flat spots" and in developing more appropriate and effective behaviors.

However, maybe you aren't one of the lucky ones who get to have such an assessment of their behaviors taken. So how can you obtain some of the same critical information so you can address unknown or misunderstood behaviors that are misaligned with the character and values you wish to embody?

A suggestion would be to think about a small group of people at work or at home that really knows you, and would be willing to give you some candid feedback. Maybe it's the same group of people you spoke with in the previous chapter. If you are having a hard time coming up with even a short list of folks who fall into that category, it may be because they fear retribution from you if they provide anything other than positive input. In that case, you may need to bend over backward to demonstrate your sincerity and desire for honest feedback, and the solemn promise to not use it against them. Let people know that you are undertaking a critical mission, one that is vital to your personal development, and that their feedback is really important.

"Character — the willingness to accept responsibility for one's own life — is the source from which self-respect springs."
— Joan Didion, on self-respect

Who Are Your Role Models?

As I mentioned at the start of this chapter, my friend Gary is one of the people I look up to, whose character I respect, and whose values and behaviors have influenced my own. Who are the people you respect, whether it's someone in your personal life or someone you've read about? Someone in the latter category for me is Sir Ernest Shackleton. He was a polar explorer at the turn of the last century who saved his men through amazing feats of bravery and endurance when his ship became trapped in sea ice. While the majority of his men camped out on the ice cap, Shackleton and a smaller group launched several lifeboats and traveled over 700 nautical miles in some of the roughest and coldest seas on the planet to find help.

To recruit men for his expedition, he published the following newspaper ad:

Men wanted for hazardous journey.
Low wages, bitter cold, long hours of complete darkness.
Safe return doubtful. Honour and recognition in the event of success.[1]

---

[1]   The 100 Greatest Advertisements, 1852–1958 by Julian Lewis Watkins

Well, sign me up…not! But the ad and his exploits speak volumes about his character traits, including bravery, adventure, honesty, and resilience. His story is still well known today because we harbor deep admiration for people with a sturdy character that holds up under the most trying circumstances. On some level, we are probably doing a self-assessment, thinking, *How would I hold up if I were in that situation?* Granted, Shackleton's trials are not the kind of thing most of us experience in life, but what about facing the unexpected death of a loved one? What about dealing with the loss of a job or a health crisis? What about needing to have a challenging discussion with a peer about their work? What about the global pandemic that we faced? While these examples are on a wide spectrum of challenging circumstances, some extreme while others are more typical, our response is still rooted in our character.

One approach to putting a finer point on the character traits you wish to develop is by thinking about people who model the traits you desire. Who are your role models? If you have some, think about what you admire about their character. Do you admire their truthfulness? Their ability to always take the right action? To never speak a disparaging word about a coworker or manager? Are there common traits among the people you admire, or do you admire different people for different reasons? Write down the traits that stand out for you, and think about how these traits align with the character and values you wish to embody.

Another way to think about it is to bring to mind people in your life who were or are negative role models. I've worked with many leaders who were determined to lead others differently than they were led. Sometimes we can learn as much from those who behave badly as those who are models of character.

High Impact Actions for Character

In order to develop the character traits required for you to fulfill your calling, here are some actions you can take to gain greater clarity or get unstuck.

Identify your top 3–5 character traits or values

If you've never done this, it can be a powerful and potentially eye-opening activity. If you've done it, but it's been a while, it will be illustrative to see how well you've embodied those traits over time or whether they have changed for you. Remember, if you aren't clear in this area, you run the risk of allowing the storms of life to throw you off course. The ones you value should support your calling and who you wish to become as a person.

⇒ **HIGH IMPACT ACTION:** There are so many listings of character traits and values on the internet, so I would encourage you to search for those terms and start by creating a list of fifteen traits that you believe would be good to develop in pursuit of your calling and to be a better, more successful, and happier human. To get your creative juices flowing, here's just a sampling of honorable traits and values you may consider adopting:

Authenticity	*Compassion*	*Leadership*
Achievement	*Continuous Learning*	*Optimism*
Accountability	*Curiosity*	*Persistence*
Adventure	*Determination*	*Resilience*
Balance	*Fearlessness*	*Spirituality*
Collaboration	*Honesty*	*Understanding*
Creativity	*Influence*	*Wisdom*

Once you've got your list of fifteen, then look them over and narrow the list to ten.

Then, narrow the list once more to five. Yes, this is hard! But it will force you to think about those values that are most important to you. How do you want to be known and remembered? Which traits are ABSOLUTELY ESSENTIAL to living an inspired life? I call these your *Five to Thrive*. I settled on five because it's a reasonable number (not too few and not too many) and because it's easy to remember.

Write down your list of Five to Thrive, and put it where you can see it every day. On your desk. On your bathroom mirror. In a reminder that pops up on your phone at the same time every day. Keep them at the forefront of your mind and use them as a guide throughout the day. When presented with choices, actions, or decisions, think about which course of action best represents the five values that are most important to you.

Building a character workout plan

Many people put a lot of effort into developing personal exercise plans and routines to help them achieve their fitness goals. Why not use the same approach for exercising your character?

Our actions can usually be boiled down into two categories: behaviors and tasks. Tasks are what we do, and behaviors are how we do it.

⇒ **HIGH IMPACT ACTION:** To translate your Five to Thrive into action, identify the behaviors and tasks that will allow you to demonstrate those character traits. Tasks are *what you do*, and behaviors are *how you do it*. Both of these categories are equally important: for example, a clinician may be competent at drawing a patient's blood (TASK), but if they are gruff and curt with the patient (BEHAVIOR), then they aren't doing a great job. I work with lots of technically competent leaders who are brilliant when it comes to the Xs and Os of their job but are lousy leaders of people. I love it when I get to develop those folks through workshops and coaching because behaviors can be learned, and the impact these changes can have on leaders (and their people) is why I do what I do.

What behaviors and tasks will help you demonstrate the character traits and values you aspire to? If optimism is one of your desired traits, think of ways you can manifest that. Maybe you can choose to be positive when life throws you a curve. You can work on your self-talk, so instead of thinking, *Why me?* you can change it to *Why not me, and what can I learn from this?* If one of your five is persistence and your calling is to become a leader in your chosen field of work, what will you do each day to develop the knowledge or skills needed to succeed at that next level? (Which would also demonstrate the value of continuous learning.)

A friend of mine recently lost his spouse to a long and devastating illness. Instead of feeling sorry for himself, he got involved in a grief support group through his church and is grateful for the new friendships and support he's received. He is now giving back to others who are new to the group and dealing with their losses. He's not only demonstrating optimism, but he is also developing the quality of resilience at the same time.

So, for each of your Five to Thrive, think about behaviors and tasks that will allow you to demonstrate those qualities and build those muscles.

"Character cannot be developed in ease and quiet. Only through experience of trial and suffering can the soul be strengthened, vision cleared, ambition inspired, and success achieved."
— Helen Keller

Pick an accountability buddy

I see it all the time in training classes. People leave excited and fired up to put the new skills they've learned into practice. But then something happens to them when they leave the class! Emails, meetings, the crisis du jour all conspire to throw people back into old behaviors, and the worthy objective of applying what they've learned falls by the wayside.

So, one of the ways we combat that tendency is to pair people up into what I call "Accountability Buddies." Accountability buddies share their personal commitments with each other and have regular check-ins where they share how things are going, what successes they've had, and what ongoing challenges they face. It's a powerful way to create personal responsibility for yourself and to help a peer along the same journey.

⇒ **HIGH IMPACT ACTION:** Once you've identified your Five to Thrive and the behaviors and tasks you are committed to demonstrating, think about picking a partner who is committed to your success and will be willing to support you on the journey. It could be a colleague at work, a friend, or even a family member. The important thing is that they are supportive of your success and have your best interests in mind.

My Accountability Buddy is: _____

Once you've identified and contacted your buddy, share what you're up to and how they can support you. Feel free to ask how you may also be able to support them, as most people have either professional or personal development goals and could use an accountability partner too. Then mutually agree on a meeting schedule that works for both of you. The meetings can be done in person or by phone, and don't need to take more than 10–15 minutes. I would recommend they occur at least once per month for at least six months. If preferred, you can make it a group of three, which can add to the richness of the experience and up the ante on the learning.

Here's a sample template you can use for this process if you wish.

Five to Thrive	Behaviors and Tasks	Accountability Buddy	Next Meeting Date/Time
1	- -		
2	- -		
3	- -		
4	- -		
5	- -		

The One Thing to Remember Even if You Forget Everything Else in This Chapter: HAVE INTEGRITY!

Character is revealed in your thoughts and actions and is reinforced each time you take action or make a decision that is aligned with who you wish to be. Even those times when no one is looking! Be a person who always does the next right thing, and watch your inspiration soar!

CHAPTER 3

The Third C: Capability
Embracing a learner's mindset

Some years ago, I made a decision to up my level of physical fitness, since I noticed the pounds slowly gathering around my middle as I got a bit older. At first, I began a running program, which I enjoyed, but was soon looking for more of a challenge. As a result, I started signing up for road races—5Ks at first then 10Ks. I loved having goals to shoot for, and it gave me the motivation to keep up the training regimen.

Then I read about a triathlon taking place in Hampton Beach, New Hampshire. The race consisted of a half-mile swim, a 25-mile bike ride, and a 10K run. Not a full Ironman but more than enough to challenge me, and I decided to go for it.

For three months, I trained like crazy: Swimming at the YMCA pool at 6:30 in the morning, running at lunch, and going for long bike rides after work. I invested in new running shoes, a bike helmet, and several books to read on how to train to do your best in these types of races. By the time race day arrived, I was supremely confident that I had done all I could to learn and prepare, and while I held no illusions about winning, I thought I could finish in the top half of the pack.

I drove to Hampton Beach the day before the event to check in to my hotel, and to finalize my race preparations. One of the items mentioned in the race pamphlet was the strong suggestion to bring or rent a wetsuit for the swim portion of the race. Even though it was August, the Atlantic is always cold this far north (55 degrees) so a wetsuit was an important addition to my race gear.

I had prearranged to rent a wetsuit at a dive shop across from the beach, and when I stopped by that afternoon to pick it up, the owner asked me if I'd ever worn a wetsuit before and if not, would I like instructions on how to put it on? Well, I took one look at it—a one-piece rubber suit with a long zipper—and I smiled smugly and said, "No thanks, I think I can figure it out." He wished me good luck, and I went on my way.

The race began at 9:00 am the next morning, and it was clear and crisp. When I was putting my wetsuit on at the beach that morning, I noted the zipper was weirdly long but didn't give it a second thought as I zipped up the front of the suit. (Mistake #1)

When the race was almost ready to start, I gathered with the group of several hundred racers who were on the beach. I thought that it might be advantageous for me to work my way up towards the front of the pack since the swim leg wasn't my strong suit, and I wanted to get every advantage I could. I didn't ask any of the more experienced racers whether this was a good strategy or not. I just did it. (Mistake #2)

As we all stood there stretching, jumping on our toes, and itching to go, I noticed out of the corner of my eye a racer next to me eyeing me. Very casually, he said to me, "Nice wetsuit." I took a good look at myself, silently agreeing with his assessment as I voiced a simple and humble, "Thanks." Then without skipping a beat, he said, "Do you know you have it on backwards?" Suddenly it dawned on me why the zipper was so long, and I thought about quickly taking the suit off and putting it on the right way. Right at that time, the starter announced over the bullhorn, "One minute to race time!" So, I had no choice but to swim with the suit on backward.

Soon after that, the gun sounded, and I dove into the water to begin the swim. A nanosecond later, two problems developed. First, the suit began to fill with water in weird places around my joints, which caused me to start losing buoyancy. Then, all the faster racers behind me literally began swimming *over* me, and it was all I could do while taking kicks to the face and head to move to the outside lane, and like a slow-moving car with the emergency flashers on, watch myself fall further and further behind.

I did manage to finish the race, finishing in 225th place out of 228 entrants…and two racers disqualified!

After the race I sheepishly returned the wetsuit to the dive shop. The owner was there as usual and enthusiastically asked, "So, how did things go?" I thought about being honest and owning up to my foolishness but instead forced a thin smile and said, "Things couldn't have went better!"

As I reflected on this experience, I realized that it only took the mistake of thinking I knew it all to throw away months of preparation and hard work. From that point forward, I resolved to embrace a learner's mindset; to be humble enough to realize I may not know it all, to be curious in all things, and to be willing to let go of old ideas in order to adopt new, more powerful ones. I don't always succeed, but my changed mindset has made a world of difference in my life and helped me to acquire the capabilities required to fulfill my calling and live an inspired life.

Learn... Or Become Irrelevant

It seems obvious that in order to fulfill our calling and live a practically inspired life, we need to grow our capacity through the acquisition of new knowledge or skills because having the will without the skill is a guaranteed recipe for frustration and disappointment. But it's not always as easy or straightforward as it sounds.

Like my triathlon example, sometimes we think we know all we need to know when we really don't. In those instances, we need to rigorously challenge our assumptions and learn to be curious by asking ourselves the question, "What is there for me to learn or rediscover here?" Adopting this mindset keeps us open to new ideas and willing to see how they may support our growth and development.

It's critical that we remain on guard and vigilant about thoughts that may sabotage our willingness and ability to learn and grow. Often we can wish to rest on our laurels, become smugly self-satisfied with our progress, or simply wish to coast for a while. It's important to remember, however, that coasting can only take us in one direction—downhill! Most companies I work with these days are focused on developing a culture of learning and continuous improvement, and we need to create the same micro-culture in our own lives.

Our son has played baseball all his life, and when he was a senior in high school, the team he played on was really good, with several Major League Baseball candidates on the squad who were solid in pitching, hitting, and defense. The year started out with the squad winning most of their games, with a growing number of MLB scouts present at each game. The team was essentially proving the pundits right and, without fully realizing it, began to buy into the hype. As the boys began to get a little cocky and overconfident, they started slacking off just a bit in practice, losing a little of their edge in the process.

The coaches noticed this and quickly convened a team meeting. They called the team out on this behavior and challenged each player to raise their game, to get a little bit better every day. Going forward, it wasn't just about winning, but did they play better than they did the game before? Throwing down the gauntlet in this manner provided the necessary elixir to propel the team to its first-ever state championship that year. More importantly, those boys learned a valuable lesson in the importance of hard work, focus, and continuous improvement.

Learning at the Speed of Change

Back in the late '70s, there was no such thing as the internet or instantaneous communication. If you wanted to send a message from one company to another, the technology used was telex, which was sent using big, bulky machines that transmitted at around 50 baud, or approximately 66 words per minute. At that rate, it could take around five minutes to send a one-page letter. The telex industry had existed for almost 100 years, with players such as Western Union, RCA, and TRT (Tropical Radio and Telephone)—the major players. Companies often employed telex operators, whose primary job was the sending and receiving of messages.

Then came a new technology that threatened to disrupt the entire industry—fax. Fax technology was able to transmit between 2400 and 9600 baud, which blew the doors off telex speed. Also, the footprint required for a fax machine compared to a telex machine was infinitesimally smaller, and no specialized operators were required.

The old-time players in the telex industry weren't worried. "No one is going to want to get rid of their telex machines," they said. Well, guess what? Within five years, telex was gone and fax was king. An industry that had existed for almost a century was eliminated.

At the time, some thought that fax would be the dominant technology for the next 100 years. But let me ask you this…when was the last time you sent or received a fax? Something else came along within ten years that made fax largely irrelevant—something called email. And email is now being replaced by IMing and texting.

This type of disruption is even more prevalent today. Entire industries can come and go in the blink of an eye, advantages in products or solutions that used to last years may last a few weeks or months. The pace and scale of change, driven in large part by technology and the internet, is unprecedented.

The implications for the rest of us are profound, and one of those implications is that the acquisition of new knowledge is paramount, as is the letting go of old ideas or ways of doing things that are obsolete, or soon will be.

"I have no special talent. I am only passionately curious"
— Albert Einstein

Are You a Learner or Learned? Do a Checkup From the Neck Up

Our brains are remarkable organs, capable of amazing feats and abilities that are too numerous to mention here. But when it comes to learning new information and discarding old ideas, sometimes our brains can get in the way.

I'm no neuroscientist, but as I understand it, how our brains treat incoming information changes as we age. When we are children, information is received and makes impressions on our young brains, almost like droplets of water leaving shallow indentions into wet clay. Over time, as more and more information is received and processed, our brains continue to categorize information while trying to make the best use of it, and the information droplets leave deeper and deeper impressions.

Continuing with the metaphor, eventually, what were small indentations become more like canyons, and people who study this sort of thing suggest that we have reached the point where we have developed "rivers of thinking." When it comes to these rivers, there is both good news and bad news.

First, the good news. Developing these rivers of thinking is what creates expertise and helps us extract order from the world. For example, think about how you drive your car now compared to when you were first learning to drive. What used to feel like an overwhelming number of decisions and actions to take (Turn the key! Adjust your mirrors! Watch for pedestrians!) most of us now do semi-automatically. It would be hard to function normally in the world without this capability.

But when it comes to learning new things, there is some bad news. Once we have reached this point in our lives, neuroscientists would say we have less neuroplasticity, or brain flexibility. Others might say we have become stuck in our ways, which drives us to defend old ideas or beliefs when what is required for growth expanded capability is the willingness to learn new ideas and knowledge and get rid of the old. Building capability in the pursuit of our calling is dependent on our ability to do this. It's about the willingness to follow a process whereby we discover, we develop, and we discard.

The Power of Stretch

Committing to lifelong learning is an important key to fulfilling your calling and living an inspired life. It may often feel uncomfortable, but that discomfort is a sign of progress.

Recently I attended a baseball game with my wife and son, arriving twenty minutes or so before the first pitch. As we settled into our seats, I noticed several players on the field completing their pre-game warm-ups with a variety of muscle stretches. Very slowly and deliberately, they worked a number of major muscle groups: hamstrings, quads, lats, and even wrists and fingers. These players, as well as most trainers and coaches in any sport, recognize that a critical factor in achieving peak performance and avoiding debilitating injuries is a regular program of stretching.

Stretching—mentally and emotionally—is also important to the rest of us if we wish to achieve higher levels of satisfaction, success, and the benefits of an inspired life. One way we stretch is by opening ourselves to expanded or new ways of looking at the world and current trends, by getting curious about other people who may see things differently than we do, and by challenging the assumptions we make. As Oliver Wendell Holmes so eloquently stated, "A mind, once stretched to a new idea, never returns to its original dimensions."

While this may be true of ideas, it isn't always true of new skills or behaviors. Quite frequently, if we wish to adopt more empowering, robust, or inspiring actions, what is required is repeated stretching—doing something once or twice is not enough.

Several years ago, I underwent shoulder surgery, which was followed by months of physical therapy and rehabilitation. So much fun! As I worked with my therapist, he kept pushing the limits of my shoulder a little bit further, then a little bit more, then even further. The issue was that by the time I returned home, my shoulder was no longer able to return to the levels of stretch I achieved with the therapist. It took weeks and months of commitment and hard work to get my shoulder back to where it needed to be.

Learning and then applying new skills, behaviors, or approaches is no different. We may attend a training class or read a blog that gets us fired up to put the new ideas into practice, but if we don't commit to a plan for doing so, we will soon return to our old ways of being and doing.

Get a Coach or Mentor

The other relevant point regarding my physical therapy experience was that all my growth and progress was achieved by going past the point of discomfort. Just reaching the limit of my comfort zone wasn't sufficient to produce meaningful gains. I realized that I couldn't take myself past that point alone. I needed a therapist—a coach, if you will—to push me farther than I thought I could go. The same thing happened to me when I took my Outward Bound wilderness course. I realized that most of my limitations were self-imposed, and it took another person (coach, expedition leader, fill in the blank) to push me, to challenge me, to believe in me, to inspire me.

So, think about who you can enlist in support of your journey to practical inspiration. It should be someone whom you admire or has more knowledge or experience than you have. Maybe it's the Accountability Buddy you identified in the previous chapter. Or it could be a manager, a peer, or a friend, but it needs to be someone who understands your goals and your capabilities and can encourage you through feedback, reinforcement, and high impact questions that encourage you to stretch and grow.

Growth is often painful and can produce fear: Fear that we won't be successful, fear that we won't be able to do or sustain it, fear that we may appear less than bulletproof to others. However, if you push past that pain and fear, you've just punched your ticket to higher levels of performance, satisfaction, and inspiration. Just remember the power of stretch, and get ready to enjoy a stronger, more flexible, more inspired you!

> *"The great thing in the world is not so much where we stand,*
> *as in what direction we are moving."*
> — Oliver Wendell Holmes

High Impact Actions for Capability

Here are some practical ways you can build the capability you require for lasting success and inspiration.

Capture a list of "Can Do" traits you need to develop

If you want to move into a more impactful and inspired life, what are the capabilities you need to acquire to make that a reality? I think of these as your "Can Do" abilities, which can be further separated into what many refer to as soft skills and hard skills. Hard skills are things that can be measured, such as being able to use a particular programming language, drive a car, or speak a second language. These are things it's hard to fake your way through! What hard skills do you need to acquire or further develop to achieve your goals?

Soft skills are harder to quantify but no less important in most roles. These are often referred to as competencies and may include traits and behaviors such as problem-solving, team building, or communication.

⇒ **HIGH IMPACT ACTION:** Think about the role or job you aspire to, or the job you currently have but want to get better at. Then ask yourself, "What skills or competencies do I need to acquire or develop to succeed and live a more inspired life?" Brainstorm a list of ideas as a starting point, then narrow the list to a manageable number (say, seven or less). Think about how these connect to your Five to Thrive that you identified in the previous chapter. Use all the resources at your disposal to develop your list, then validate it with your Accountability Buddy. Use the following template for your work.

Competency or Skill	Why it's important	How will I develop it?	By when?

Make a regular commitment

Once you've identified what capability you need to work on, work backward from your "By when" date to come up with a set of weekly or monthly actions you can take to reach your capacity goals. Decide what is realistic in terms of when and how much time you can commit to these endeavors. Aiming too high may set you up for discouragement and failure, while aiming too low may fail to build enough momentum, challenge, and excitement to keep your eyes on the prize.

When I decided to write this book, I committed to a regular daily practice of writing and research, with goals to write one chapter a month. There were also other capabilities I needed to acquire, including learning about book editing and publishing, talking to other writers to learn how they succeeded, and reading books about becoming an author. By dedicating set times on both a daily and a weekly basis, I was able to keep the momentum going, get more excited and inspired about the journey, and meet my commitments.

I also used my Accountability Buddy to keep me on track. Knowing I was going to have to be accountable to someone for the commitments I was making to myself often provided the kick in the pants I needed on those days when I just didn't feel like doing it.

⇒ **HIGH IMPACT ACTION:** Put a finer level of detail into the last two columns from the table you just developed, namely actions you will take and by when. If your schedule fluctuates a bit and it's difficult to make a daily commitment, set up a weekly one. Try to be detailed and include the use of SMART criteria, if possible. SMART goals are Specific, Measurable, Actionable, Realistic, and Time-Bound.

Find a mentor

A mentor is someone who has knowledge, skills, or experience that you don't, but would like to acquire. This person could be your Accountability Buddy, or it could be a different person altogether. Who it is isn't as important as what they bring to the table experience-wise, and their willingness to devote some time with you regularly. The best mentoring relationships become real relationships, where they take an interest in your success, enjoy answering questions and providing information, and may even leverage their connections to further your development.

Maybe you're already thinking of someone who would be a good mentor for you. Maybe no one is coming to mind at all. That's okay! But start thinking about people who are doing the kind of work you want to do, who share your values and may be willing to help out. If there's no one in your current network that fits the bill, cast a wider net by asking your coworkers, friends, or family for ideas on who may be a potential mentor for you. Then maybe they can make the introduction so you can have an initial conversation with that person.

Remember, first impressions matter, so always be respectful but clear in what you are asking for, why you think the potential mentor would be a good match, and what it would mean to you if they said yes. Most people, if approached in such a way, are more than happy to lend a helping hand and may even get as much out of the relationship as you do.

The key to developing a long-term relationship is to honor your commitments, don't misuse their time, and try to incorporate any suggestions they make.

⇒ **HIGH IMPACT ACTION:** Make a list of people who fit the mentor criteria that are important to you. Create this list by thinking about your contacts and by reaching out and asking others whom you trust for recommendations. Once assembled, prioritize the list then write out what you will say when you speak to them about being your mentor. Remember to focus on why you think they are a good match, what you'd like to learn from them, and how their expertise and guidance would benefit you.

My List of Potential Mentors

Who	Why they would be a great mentor for me

The One Thing to Remember Even if You Forget Everything Else in This Chapter: EMBRACE YOUR UNIQUENESS!

It's a fool's errand to constantly compare yourself to others because there's always someone you'll come up short to. Instead, focus on your unique attributes and build on your strengths to develop greater capability. Don't let what may appear to be a long road ahead get you down. Self-pity is a surefire way to lose momentum and eventually throw in the towel. Catch yourself in the act of doing something right and build on those successes!

CHAPTER 4

The Fourth C: Curiosity
Pay attention and see what shows up

Jody is my bride of over 29 years, and I'm the luckiest guy in the world to be her husband, best friend, and confidante as we travel through this life. A big chunk of the credit goes to her, as well as to my dumb luck to have the good sense to ask her to marry me way back when. Whether it's picking a spouse or a new hire, a significant ingredient to a long, fruitful partnership is to choose the right person in the first place.

Paul and Jody in our younger days

For us, the second ingredient is the willingness to invest time and effort into the relationship. We believe that is especially true when you've been together for a long time, simply because it's too easy to take each other for granted and to grow apart as the years advance. We've seen this time and time again where friends or acquaintances separate or divorce once they become empty nesters, often after over twenty years of marriage. As one friend told me, "Soon after the kids left home, I woke up one morning realizing that I didn't know who my wife was anymore."

So, in a mutual effort to not let that happen to us, we regularly spend time together doing a variety of activities, sometimes things she enjoys and sometimes things I enjoy. But we also make a regular habit of trying new things and creating new experiences for ourselves, of understanding the benefits of expanding our worldview while having fun that bonds us together as a couple. So that we will always remember this ethos, we have a sign over our bedroom door which reads, *Love is Being Stupid Together* (having a sense of humor and not taking yourselves too seriously helps, too). I remind her of this whenever I pull up the Karaoke Channel and, in my off-key way, belt out something by Ed Sheerin, Taylor Swift, or Tom Jones.

Despite my commitment to trying new things, I nearly gagged on my tuna salad sandwich when Jody suggested over lunch that we sign up for ballroom dancing lessons. I gagged in large part because, for most of my adult life, whenever I got the urge to dance, I lay down on the sofa until the feeling passed. If I unavoidably found myself in a situation that required "dancing," I would dust off a collection of somewhat convulsive moves Jody calls "Driving the Bus." Try and picture this, if you dare: A middle-aged man, both hands gripping an invisible wheel while rocking side to side, occasionally signaling for a left or right turn. I thought this was a pretty good imitation of "dancing," however, after a few minutes of this, an embarrassed Jody would helpfully propose, "Might I suggest that you just stop doing that?"

So back to the dance lessons. Sensing my unease, Jody proceeded to sell me on the idea. "First, we're only committing to one lesson. That's it. Second, keep an open mind; it may be fun!" The last time she asked me to keep an open mind was when I was selected to run an all-hands company meeting, which only opened the door for me to completely change careers and geography, ultimately leading me to the inspired life of my dreams. So, it was for this reason I agreed to give it a try. But a part of me was also curious about learning to dance, and I was interested in getting a taste of it.

When we arrived for our lesson, we met our instructor, Kharyton, a twenty-something émigré from Ukraine. Kharyton had an engaging smile, a quick wit, and put us at ease immediately. Over the next forty minutes, he took us through a series of dances, including the Rumba, Tango, and the Waltz. I learned what a box step was, how to strike the proper posture for the Tango, and that I always had to escort my lady by the arm while in the studio.

Much to my shock and surprise, the lesson was more than tolerable; it was downright enjoyable! I was enjoying it because the act of dancing provided a moderate aerobic activity that Jody and I could do together. I was enjoying it because I was actually grasping what they were trying to teach us and could demonstrate some of it at a basic level, making real progress in a short amount of time. But mostly, I was enjoying it because I was experiencing the challenge and thrill of learning something entirely new, which vitalized and engaged me while developing new neural pathways in my brain. I soon realized it would have been a shame if my initial close-mindedness had prevented us from having this experience. As had happened in the past, I was reminded that curiosity and openness always trump inertia and false or outdated assumptions.

Our initial experience was so positive that we signed up for several more months of lessons, met some wonderful people, and experienced an introduction into a dancing subculture we didn't know existed. Now when we go out, I can hit the dance floor with a modicum of confidence, and while we're not exactly *Dancing with the Stars* material, we are enjoying our new skill sets and more reasons to spend fun times together.

Curious People Challenge Their Assumptions

Do you know curious people? If so, think about how they show up differently than other people you know or interact with. Do they ask interesting questions that force you to think? Do they demonstrate verbally or non-verbally that they are listening to what you have to say? Do you leave interactions with them feeling challenged, reflective, or enriched?

For starters, curious people are interested in what they can learn or discover, rather than sharing what they already know in order to impress others (or themselves). Some of the best leaders I've had the opportunity to work with have developed this special quality. They ask more than they tell, they listen and pay attention, and they make the interaction about you, not them. They don't do this because it's a nice thing to do, they do this so they can learn things they might otherwise not learn.

Curious people suck up knowledge like vacuum cleaners, and they seek out learning from everyone and everything they encounter. Unlike my story of the triathlon and wetsuit I shared earlier, they evaluate each situation they encounter to see if there is something new to learn or discover, or a different way to react at that moment than they may have reacted in the past. They start with a clean slate and don't let outdated or erroneous assumptions or beliefs hold them back. They look for the uniqueness in each moment they experience.

Assumptions aren't always a bad thing; they can often be our friends. Assumptions can help us make sense of the world, either consciously or unconsciously. For instance, when we're driving and we approach a green light, we keep going under the assumption that the cross-street drivers will stop (occasionally, this can be a faulty assumption). When it comes to situations that require more judgment or curiosity, many of us process the present moment by filtering it through our assumptions or beliefs. The difficulty arises when we continue to operate from long-held assumptions even when they are roadblocks to our success and happiness.

As an example, if we believe that there's no point in trying to manage a self-defeating behavior because we've tried to do so in the past but have failed, then our belief will likely manifest as reality, and our limiting belief will be reinforced. The good news is that the opposite is also true: If we believe we are capable and can do what we've set our mind to do, that belief often provides the necessary remedy to create that reality for us and reinforce that positive self-image.

In the corporate world, there's an adage that the culture of an organization is more important than whatever strategies may be deployed, no matter how brilliant. What this means is that if the employees of that company don't believe in the strategy, or don't believe they can successfully contribute to it, then that limiting belief usually dooms those strategies—and individuals—to failure.

I like to use the analogy of a rowing team. When I lived in Boston, I loved to run or take walks along the Charles River, and would often see the university rowing teams practicing on the river. Despite hours and hours of practice, what if on the day of the regatta they look across the river to their competition and think, "Boy, there's no way we're going to beat them. Look at how big and strong they are. We don't stand a chance." Well, if that's the belief of most of those team members, then they're probably right, and their beliefs will probably create that outcome.

Developing a positive mindset and constantly evaluating the assumptions you make about situations, others, or yourself makes it easier for you to stay curious and acquire the knowledge and capabilities you need for success and inspiration. Decide to become aware of the self-talk or chatter that goes on in your head all the time, and decide whether those messages are worth keeping or should be changed. No one else is responsible for your thoughts and feelings but you.

> *"If you think you can, or think you can't...you're right."*
> — Henry Ford

Curiosity Is the Path to the Stretch Zone

I like to think of consciousness as an island in a sea of mystery. As we acquire new knowledge or ideas, our island expands and grows...but so too does the shoreline where we meet the unknown. To a certain extent, the more we learn, the less we know. Or at least we become more aware of what we don't know.

This idea shows up with people we live or work with. Some know what they don't know, and some don't know what they don't know. The latter category describes a state of ignorance that is difficult to break out of without the intervention of some type of external event to help these people shift from ignorance to not-knowing-ness. Once you achieve not-knowing-ness, when you know that you don't know, that awareness can provide the necessary elixir to gain the knowledge, ideas, or experience needed to close critical gaps. Asking others for their input or feedback (as described in Chapter Two) is also an effective way to reduce your blind spots and identify areas for new knowledge or ideas to create a different reality for yourself.

Another way to break out of this trap is to use your curiosity to seek out new experiences that challenge your current thinking or knowledge, and serve to expand your consciousness shoreline. The dance lessons I detailed earlier in this chapter opened up a new world to me, and they reinforced the criticality of stepping out of our comfort zones and stretching our minds to new ideas. Not only is this crucial as we age to support brain function, but they create knowledge reservoirs that we can call upon in the future as we work to live an inspired life.

My Outward Bound experience did that for me, by staying with the curiosity to see how I would respond to a myriad of challenges. Waking up at 4:00 am and jumping into the icy Atlantic from a galley boat, learning to navigate open ocean using primitive tools and leading a diverse group of individuals under trying conditions expanded my capability and opened me up to more effective ways of being and working. Lessons I learned during this 28-day experience have stayed with me almost thirty years later, and I think about this experience whenever I hesitate when presented with an opportunity to encounter something new or challenging.

At work, there is a balance to be struck when seeking out or being presented with stretch assignments. Finding the proper degree of stretch is the key to a successful experience and the development of expanded capability.

If the opportunity doesn't provide ample stretch, it can lead to boredom fairly quickly. For instance, if you're always the go-to person in your department for a particular task or assignment, what may have begun as a stretch can soon become routine.

On the other hand, opportunities that provide too much stretch can lead to feelings of overwhelm, akin to floundering in rough seas. Even these assignments can be made to be right-sized given adequate support in the form of coaching, mentoring, or other resources, but without them, we can fail or become exhausted by the experience.

Keeping your eyes open for opportunities to stretch your thinking and capabilities and staying curious during the process provides much-needed stimulation and can break us out of stale patterns, habits, and thought patterns. Seeking them out in unusual places, in addition to traditional areas, can bring unexpected and welcomed perspectives and energy.

"The only difference between a rut and a grave are the dimensions."
— Ellen Glasgow

The Power of Questions

Another observation I've made about curious people is that they are really good at asking questions—questions that are typically designed with two purposes in mind. The first purpose is to ask questions that will provide them with needed insights or allow them to understand something they don't. The second purpose is to see something through someone else's eyes, and in doing so, be able to expand their worldview and gain a broader perspective.

But good questions can also impact and create value for the person being asked the question. Open-ended questions that make you think deeply and compel you to consider impacts and implications can not only benefit the questioner, but the questioned.

The head of security for a public utility told me a story once that highlighted the power of asking questions. One day he was driving around the perimeter of one of their power plants when he noticed one of his security guards getting out of his vehicle before it had come to a complete stop, literally jumping out of the car as it rolled to a stop. This was a clear violation of safety procedures, and the leader drove over to the scene intending to read this guard the riot act—basically to put the hammer down and let him know that if that ever happened again, he would be written up and possibly fired.

But for some reason that day, the leader decided to try a different approach. "Something inside of me compelled me to ask a question instead of just yelling at the guy." So when he pulled up, he said to the guard, "I noticed that you just got out of the car before it came to a complete stop. Can you help me understand why you did that?"

Some of the possible answers to this question that I considered included a swarm of bees in the car or a failure of the brakes, but the answer was none of these. The reason why this guard jumped out of the car before it came to complete stop was that he was a war veteran who had just returned from a tour of duty in the Middle East, where it was standard procedure to jump out of Humvees before they became easy targets for insurgents.

The leader continued: "Because I asked a question instead of just hammering the guard, I learned something I probably wouldn't have learned otherwise. Now, when we hire new guards, I ask if they're veterans and if so, make a point of letting them know they don't need to jump out of the vehicles here."

Therefore, the next time you are tempted to speak more than listen or tell more than ask, stop. Try the opposite approach, and maybe you'll learn something new. Keep the image of an alligator in your mind. What does an alligator look like? Tiny ears, tiny eyes, and a BIG mouth. And if they're not careful, they get turned into shoes and handbags!

> *"I never learn anything while talking.*
> *I only learn things when I ask questions."*
> — Lou Holtz

High Impact Actions for Curiosity

Here are some practical ways you can demonstrate curiosity and reap its benefits in your life.

Get out of character more often

Do you watch the same shows on Netflix or TV all the time? Do you read the same authors or the same category of books? Do you only seek out points of view on social media that reinforce your own? When's the last time you got curious enough and learned a new skill, considered alternative viewpoints, or took a class just for the fun of it?

One way to nurture curiosity and live a more inspired life is to take advantage of opportunities to step out of character and try something new to see what you can learn or discover through the experience. Whether it's reading the classics, taking a cooking class, or volunteering at a senior center, challenge yourself to experience a broader swath of what life has to offer. Then focus on the learning you take away from the experience.

⇒ **HIGH IMPACT ACTION:** Commit to creating at least one new experience for yourself each week. Maybe it involves reading a book on a topic you've never dug into before (I recently read a book on life in the Middle Ages that gave me a completely different perspective and appreciation for that era). It could be signing up for continuing education or an online class in a subject you've never explored. Cooking, writing, painting—the list is endless, the risk is small, and the potential upside is huge. Perhaps it's joining a group like Toastmasters to work through your fear of public speaking. Whatever it is, get comfortable with being uncomfortable.

During and after the experience, use a journal to capture notes on what you learned or discovered through the experience: about the world, about others, or about yourself. Do this consistently and watch your eagerness to take on these stretch activities expand.

My new experience:

_____

_____

_____

_____

_____

_____

What did I learn from this?

_____

_____

_____

_____

_____

_____

Ask more and better questions

Fundamentally, curiosity is the process of asking questions. Whether it's an interaction with a peer at work, a family member at home, or a stranger you just met, get into the habit of asking more questions to learn about them and their points of view. Learn to ask questions that encourage the other person to open up, questions that encourage them to think deeply, questions that can create as much value for them as they do for you.

Questions that begin with *how* or *what* typically fit the bill. For example, "How did you get on this career path?" or "What did you need to learn to succeed in this new role?" One litmus test you can use to gauge the impact of your question involves the verbal or non-verbal reactions your question provokes. A good question may cause the other person to ponder quietly for a few moments, or maybe it triggers excitement and they respond at length. Someone may even say, "Boy, that's a really good question!" Get better at asking good questions and telling less, and watch your circle of influence expand and your learning soar.

⇒ **HIGH IMPACT ACTION:** Start to build a repository of questions you can use in a variety of settings and interactions. Add questions to the list that passed the litmus test described earlier. Then, refer to this list before an important meeting or discussion to see what questions you might be able to use as is, which ones you could use with some tweaking, or which new questions come to mind from reviewing your current list. Keep adding to the list as you build your questioning muscle.

Examples of effective questions include:

○ Where do you see your career in (x) years?
○ What are the top three things you learned by going through that experience?
○ What would an optimal result look like?
○ What are your most important priorities this year?
○ How do you feel about... (your work, your company, our new strategy, etc.)?

Practice active listening

The second and most important part of asking good questions is listening to the answer! Not listening to the answer is one of the issues I have with many traditional sales questioning models. While your client or prospect is responding to your last question, you're already thinking about the next question to ask, in an effort to guide the other person to the conclusion you want them to reach. This isn't active listening, it's manipulation! People can easily tell whether you're really listening to them or not. Even if you disagree with what they are saying, using the active listening technique at least lets the other person know that they've been heard (a critical human need) while allowing you to process information that will naturally lead to the next question or step in the discussion.

⇒ **HIGH IMPACT ACTION:** Practice the following active listening experiment with a colleague, friend, or family member:

Start with a question about a significant event that recently occurred in that person's life. Maybe it was an exotic vacation, or a home purchase, or a new job. Then encourage them to keep talking by using simple verbal and non-verbal techniques, such as the following:

- Nonverbal: Nodding, smiling, eye contact, open body language, giving them your complete attention.

- Verbal: Use simple probes to encourage further sharing such as, "Tell me more," or "Please go on," or "Uh-huh."

Experiment for at least five minutes. At the end, ask the person you are listening to what that experience was like for them. How did it feel to be listened to? Share what it was like for you: How did it feel to listen authentically, without an agenda or the need to steer the conversation?

Use this experience as a starting point for engaging in more active listening at work and home. Make it more about others and less about yourself and see how your curiosity muscle expands and how it changes how others perceive you.

The One Thing to Remember Even if You Forget Everything Else in This Chapter: EMBRACE CHANGE!

Change happens, whether you like it or not. Stay ahead of the curve by staying curious, trying new experiences, and learning new things. Not only will it help your career, but it will also energize and infuse your life with energy and a growth mindset. Start small to go big!

CHAPTER 5

The Fifth C: Connection
Making time for important relationships

When we first moved to Arizona, things were exciting, chaotic, and crazy. For starters, I had to adjust to living in a new location where we didn't know anyone, which was very different from the New England area that I spent my whole life in. Second, I had decided to leave the relative safety and familiarity of the corporate world and start my own speaking and training practice. There were times when I felt like there weren't enough hours in the day to do everything that needed doing to set us up for success.

Starting a new business is a powerful motivator, especially when there's no promise of a payday, and you're the sole provider of income for your family. As a result, I was frequently traveling to generate new business and revenue, and when I was home was preoccupied with doing more of the same.

At one point, I realized that I had been slacking on my dad duties and resolved to spend more time with my son Austin. Austin was four years old at the time and already into baseball big time (he would later play collegiate ball for Arizona in the Pac 12), so I thought about taking him to a baseball game.

Austin with Paul, winning a trip to the College World Series, 2016

While the local pro team, the Diamondbacks, was an option, that involved spending more money than I was interested in spending at the time. However, that particular year there was a semi-pro baseball league in Arizona, and the local team was called the Valley Vipers. Summer baseball outdoors in Phoenix probably wasn't the smartest business venture. No wonder the league folded after one year! But Austin didn't care what league we saw so long as it was baseball, so we decided to attend a Valley Vipers game the following Tuesday.

The Monday before the game, I received a call from one of the few clients I had at the time that had booked my services for the following month to conduct some leadership training. He said that due to a shift in priorities, they needed to change some dates and asked if I could fly out to work with them the next day. My immediate reaction was to accommodate this last-minute request, and I was within an eyelash of saying yes. But then I caught a glimpse of a picture of Austin and me on my desk. At that point, I heard myself saying, "No, I can't make it. I have another commitment."

When I hung up, I immediately harbored doubts about that decision. After all, I was passing up much-needed income by turning him down. However, as fate would have it, what happened at that ball game that night erased any doubts.

We went to Scottsdale Stadium for the game, us and about 500 other diehard baseball fans who were willing to sit in 100-degree heat to watch a game. To generate more fan interest, the PR folks had promotions and contests for the fans every inning, like kids racing the mascot around the bases, putting competitions on top of the dugouts, and a hitting contest for adults. They had a desk at the entrance where you could enter a name and your seat number into a fishbowl to see if your name would be drawn for one of the contests. They had one fishbowl for children's contests and one for the adult baseball hitting contest. After dropping Austin's name in the fishbowl, we started to walk away until the promotions gal said, "Sir, why don't you enter the adult contest?" I didn't want to, but Austin's eyes lit up as he said, "Come on, Dad! You can do it!" I reluctantly put my name into the bowl, secretly hoping that it wouldn't get drawn because I hadn't swung a baseball bat in years.

Sure enough, around the fourth inning, the staff member came walking toward our section, and although I tried to make myself invisible, it didn't work. She tapped me on the shoulder and said, "Congratulations! You won the chance to compete in the hitting contest." I'm thinking, *Maybe because my name was the only one in the fishbowl, huh?*

The contest would be held in between the next inning, and involved the placement of a ball on a T-ball type tee at second base, which you then had one chance to hit it over the right-field wall, over this billboard of local favorite Skippy the Clown, which was about four feet wide. And if you hit it over the sign with your one and only swing, you would win dinner at a local pizza joint. As the staff member was leading me down to the field, Austin said, "Hey Dad, can I come down to watch?" And I said, "Sure, Son!" while thinking, *Why not get an even closer look at me making a fool of myself?*

Austin stood by the rail while the woman and I walked out to second base after the inning ended. Then my name was announced and the crowd started cheering, and now I'm really feeling the pressure. The baseball looks like it's about the size of a golf ball, and the bat feels like a lead weight. As I started to swing, I half-closed my eyes and prayed, *Please, just let me hit the thing!*

Well, the miracle of miracles, I hit the ball squarely. It took off toward right field—low, but gaining elevation—and cleared the fence with about two feet to spare, right over the outstretched arms of Skippy the Clown. I felt like Robert Redford in *The Natural.* While the crowd was going crazy, I threw the bat down and high-fived the woman while shouting, "I can't believe I hit it over Skippy!" and she replied, "I know, I can't believe you hit it either!"

But here's the best part: As I turned toward the dugout, what do I see but Austin, jumping over the rail, running toward me as fast as he could. When he reached me, he leaped into my arms, gave me a great bear hug, and said, "I knew you could do it, Dad! I love you." As we're walking off the field together, the first baseman jokingly said to me, "You know, you're not so bad, we could use you out here!"

Now, here's the thing: I almost missed out on that. If I had taken the work and not gone to the game, I would have missed that special moment of connection with my son that still resonates with me so many years later.

Moments That Matter...and They All Do

Moments to connect authentically with others matter, whether it's at work, home, or in the community. People who live inspired lives understand the importance of interconnectedness and can leave impressions with people even during short interactions.

I was leading a leadership retreat several years ago when we invited a senior officer of the company to say a few words after dinner. This leader ran a sales organization for a Fortune 100 global company and had over 4,000 direct and indirect reports underneath his command.

When I was introduced to him before dinner, I was struck by how interested he was in who I was, my background, and my impressions of the group. As I later observed him interacting with others, I noticed the same behavior in action: Asking questions, listening, making comments that indicated that he was paying attention to what others were saying. He was fully present, modeling humility in its most powerful form.

This alone left me slightly incredulous. That was because, during this period, there were lots of things that were occupying his time as a global leader. Deployment of new strategies, considering possible acquisition targets, retaining key customers, and a litany of other mission-critical initiatives were all in play. Despite this whirlwind of activity, he seemed able to put all of those issues out of his mind that evening and was fully present in each interaction. He was able to stay curious, make every interaction about others, and by doing so, won or reinforced the respect of every person in that room.

This was also a good reminder to me about how people are always watching us, to see how we're showing up and whether our actions are aligned with our words, which is especially critical for people leaders, but everyone needs to be aware of it. It takes a long time to build credibility, but it can be lost very quickly.

Some people cultivate a large number of close relationships while others have fewer, but the important thing is to have some. Current research on the topic is finding that there are tangible benefits to be reaped by having connections with others, including emotional stability and longevity.

Making Deposits into Your Relationship Accounts

Few people are completely self-made successes. As I've thought about my own life and career, there have been many people who have given their time and expertise to support me, encourage me, and enlighten me, which has provided invaluable guidance and helped me become the man I am today.

Inspired people are focused less on what they can take from life and more on what they can contribute to it, and how they can help others. Some people are naturally wired to do this while others have to work at it. But doing this regularly is one of the differentiators between an inspired life and an average one. So many people are too inwardly focused and live their lives from a state of unsatisfied needs, which generates an undercurrent of fear that permeates our lives, whether we are aware of it or not. Variations include, "What if I don't get something I want?" or "What if I lose something I need?" This type of scarcity mentality leads many to make decisions and engage with others in a completely self-serving way, which is not hard for others to pick up on.

Better questions to ask ourselves is, "What can I contribute to this person (situation, etc.)?", "Can I proactively reach out to offer assistance without being asked?" and "Or do we just reach out to someone at home or work when we need something?" We've all met people like that—and we're not too fond of them. I spoke to one manager who said that when he sees a call coming in from a particularly self-serving individual, he thinks, *What do they need now?* Who wants to be perceived like that guy?

I like to think of investing in people and relationships akin to making deposits in a relationship bank account. Each time you make a call just to ask how it's going, without a me-focused agenda; every time you ask someone what you can do to help or better yet, just *help* them; whenever you put aside your agenda for someone else's, you've made a deposit in the relationship account. Whether you ever need to make a withdrawal from that account—in other words, need help or a favor from them—is not as important as developing the habit of seeking to give more than you get. Getting out of yourself and focusing on others is a surefire way to get off the pity-pot and shift your worldview from one of scarcity to one of abundance.

Now let's acknowledge that this isn't always easy to do. These types of interactions typically fall into the *Important, Not Urgent* category, which often loses out to the *Urgent, Important,* or worse to the *Urgent, Not Important* bucket. If you don't bring in your sales numbers or achieve your weekly goals (*Urgent, Important*), you may just get a call from your boss at 5:00 pm on Friday, demanding to know why. On the other hand, you probably won't get that call if you didn't reach out to help someone else or lend resources to a colleague who was in danger of missing a critical deliverable.

Therefore, the challenge we all face is to strike a balance between those things that are important and urgent, and the things that are not urgent but important. Investing in both areas is the key to lasting success, happiness, and an inspired life. Paying less attention to things that are not important, whether they are urgent or not urgent, is a good beginning.

Demonstrating an Attitude of Gratitude

The most inspired people I've met don't take their success, good fortune, or the people they work and spend time with for granted; they are authentically appreciative and always show it. However, it's not always easy to avoid falling into a sense of entitlement, and many good people fall prey to this trap.

A friend of mine relayed a story about a small startup company he worked for a few years ago. After several challenging years, they were starting to meet with some success, and at Thanksgiving, the leadership team decided to present each employee with a frozen turkey as a way of saying, "Thank you for all you've done to help us get where we are." This thoughtful gesture genuinely touched everyone, and the morale at the company had never been higher.

The turkey-giving morphed into a tradition, continuing for several more years. With each passing year, the sense of entitlement grew. "Great, another turkey," was the typical reply.

Then one year, they were facing challenging times again and decided to stop the Thanksgiving turkey giveaway. When the news was communicated, many employees were outraged. "Where's my turkey!" was one of the reactions heard in the lunchroom, as well as "I bet management's still getting *their* turkeys." What had begun as a nice perk and thoughtful gesture had evolved into entitlement, and left some employees feeling taken advantage of and on the receiving end of bad fortune.

Being able to shift to an attitude of gratitude and cultivate it on a regular basis is a great way to focus on what is right and not on what is wrong. Many people make a regular habit of writing down gratitude lists, things large and small that they are grateful for, as a tool for warding off negativity or a bad attitude. Some folks express gratitude for obvious good fortunes such as the birth of a child or grandchild, a return to good health, or a financial windfall. Others are no less grateful for the more mundane things in daily life, such as being able to take a walk on a beautiful spring day, have a roof over their heads, or simply just waking up on this side of the earth!

When my son was young, I began a tradition on Father's Day, which continued until he was a grown young man. When he would present me with my Father's Day card on those Sunday mornings,

I would present him with a letter I wrote to him. The letter would express how proud I was of all he had achieved but, more importantly, who he was becoming, and my gratitude for getting the opportunity to be his dad. I'm not sure they meant a great deal to him at the time, but my wife told me he saved every one. Someday, if he is fortunate to become a father himself, maybe he will look back at these letters and continue the tradition with his son or daughter.

High Impact Actions for Connection

Here are some actions you can take to deepen your connection to others in your life.

Less screen time, more people time

Technology is a great tool, but we can get too wrapped up in it and miss opportunities to spend time directly with others at home or work. Becoming aware of how much time you spend on your devices is the first step in changing that behavior, so you can repurpose that time by spending it with others.

⇒ **HIGH IMPACT ACTION:** There are a variety of applications on the market that will track how many times a day you pick up your phone and how many hours a day you are using it. Find one that works with your device and start using it to log your screen time. Once you have a sense of the average time spent on your device, then set a goal for reducing that time. Be realistic and start by making incremental progress. Maybe instead of three hours a day, your intermediate goal will be to reduce that to two hours a day, with the ultimate goal of getting to one hour per day. I'm not suggesting you reduce work time you use your device for, but time-wasters like social media or gaming are good places to start.

Develop the art of storytelling

Some of the most inspired and effective people I've worked with are adept at being able to tell a good story. Stories help bring data to life, provide examples to follow, or anchor important learnings that people will remember. Stories also connect us to others and help others relate to us in meaningful ways.

Best practices for storytelling include the following:

- Choose a story your audience can relate to
- Focus the story on one core message
- Provide enough details to bring the story to life
- Keep it concise
- End with clear learning or a call to action

Self-deprecating stories (showing how you messed up but learned from it) are always preferable to stories where you come off as the hero (not much humility in that).

⇒ **HIGH IMPACT ACTION:** Identify an opportunity to use a story at work to communicate an important concept or reinforce an important takeaway. A good story can be told in three to five minutes, so don't feel like you have to write a twelve-act play. Once written, practice telling the story to a trusted friend or colleague. Refine based on feedback before using it in a work or other setting.

If this is an area that you would like to explore further, I suggest finding a Toastmasters group you could join. Toastmasters was a critical step in my development as a public speaker. Whether you want to take that path in your career or not, the lessons learned and experience gained in Toastmasters will help you in all areas of your life that require communication.

Make a practice of gratitude

As previously mentioned, an attitude of gratitude is a powerful tool for living an inspired life. Whether gratitude is a feeling that comes naturally to you or not, it can always be developed further by the application of some simple exercises. Like the adage says, fake it 'til you make it!

⇒ **HIGH IMPACT ACTION:** Buy a blank journal or use your notes function on your phone to capture at least three things you are grateful for each day. Some people like to do this at the beginning of their day while others prefer to do it at the end, but the important thing is to just do it. As you do this for a while, take time to reflect on your entries whenever you're feeling fearful or overwhelmed. This practice will help you reconnect with all the good things in your life and redirect your thinking.

You can also make a point of calling or visiting one person a week just to say hello, and to express your gratitude for their presence in your life. Maybe you're grateful for their friendship, or for something they went out of their way to help you with. Maybe you just want to check in because they're important in your life and you want them to know that. My friend Gary, who passed away at a young age, made a practice of making phone calls to friends and family during his commute home from work. Instead of being frustrated with traffic or worried about work, he focused on connection to others and expressing his gratitude for them. Think about the power of making a similar shift in your own life!

The One Thing to Remember Even if You Forget Everything Else in This Chapter: PUT YOURSELF IN ANOTHER'S SHOES!

The best way to connect with others is to be able to see the world through their eyes. Often, we judge people exhibiting negative behavior as being out of touch or a jerk, when, in fact, we don't know what issues or pain they may be dealing with in their life. Build the capacity to be empathetic, to be less distracted when engaged with others, and do the little things that separate you from most: Remember people's names (and use them), ask how they are doing (and mean it), offer a kind word or support (and mean that, also). Taking these actions gets you out of your head and will build stronger connections with the people in your life.

CHAPTER 6

The Sixth C: Centeredness
Maintaining balance and perspective

Some years ago, when I was on the routine speaking circuit, I found myself making my way through an airport to make a connecting flight when someone walking in my direction stopped dead in their tracks. We made eye contact as he racked his brain for where he knew me from, while I clearly had no idea who he was. Finally, he smiled, pointed at me, and excitedly claimed, "You're the guy!" Not being sure what to say to that, I replied, "Well, maybe."

Delivering a keynote address, 2008

He continued. "No, you're the guy who spoke at our national sales meeting a few months ago. In Miami, remember?" Yes, now I remembered and acknowledged that yes, indeed, *I am the guy*. At that, he took my hand, pumped it vigorously, and exclaimed, "Man, you were the best speaker we had!" A smile came to my face as I stood a little taller and thought, *Boy, I really AM making a difference to people!* Visions of speaking in arenas to 60,000 people, appearances on *Oprah*, and houses on both coasts flashed before my eyes. Then my new friend paused for what seemed an eternity. Finally, he sheepishly inquired, "What was it you spoke about again?"

In that moment, my heart sank. Really, he can't remember my topic? It was only several months ago! But then I had a moment of clarity and realized the universe had just sent me a dose of much-needed humility. The humility to not take myself so seriously, to be happy that at least the guy remembered me and that maybe I needed to make some changes to my work to ensure that people were not only entertained but took away some valuable knowledge and tools that would create real impact at work and home. In a few short minutes, I had gone from elation to deflation to "right size," and I silently expressed my gratitude for the grace needed to gain the proper perspective and centeredness.

The Importance of Being Centered

What does it mean to be centered? When you Google the definition of "centered," it reads, "Being placed or situated in the center." I think of a dot in the middle of a circle, being equidistant from all points on the circle. From a human perspective, the opposite of being centered is being out of balance, where you're devoting too much time and energy to one area of your life and not enough to others.

Let's look at the different categories that constitute human life. My top categories include work, family, personal health, spirituality, fun, and friendships. For others, the categories may be different. Whatever your categories are, do you strive to maintain an appropriate balance between them? Or do you find yourself devoting too much time to one area at the expense of others? Perhaps you work long hours, or have a growing family, or are a caregiver to a loved one. In those cases, it can seem impossible to create a balanced life. But we should always aim to improve, to seek progress (not perfection) because the costs of an unbalanced life are real and can be severe.

Chronic stress is the most obvious manifestation of an unbalanced life. While some stress in our lives is good (it can provide focus and intentionality), chronic stress is unequivocally bad.

According to changingminds.org, some of the workplace costs of stress include:

- 60–80% of worksite accidents are the result of stress
- Costs associated with stress may reduce US industry profits by 10%
- 75–90% of visits to physicians are stress-related
- Cost to US industry of stress-related illnesses is over $200 billion a year
- 20% of the total number of healthcare claims are stress-related
- 16% of healthcare costs are explained by stress[1]

Lack of centeredness, which results in stress, is an epidemic that has real costs to individuals and organizations. So, what can we do about it?

What Is Within Your Control?

There are events in our lives that cause us to become unbalanced and stressed, but is it often our reaction to these events that compounds the stress. For example, many people I work with feel overwhelmed and out of balance at work. And in today's environment, it's easy to see why. We live in an age of constant and never-ending change, rapid disruption, and a high degree of uncertainty. Some have adopted the acronym VUCA (originally coined by the military to describe battlefield conditions) to describe the world we live and work in: Volatile, Uncertain, Complex, and Ambiguous. Sometimes it can feel like we're trying to change the tire on a moving car. In a corporate setting, reorganizations, reductions in force, mergers and acquisitions, and changes in roles and responsibilities are byproducts

---

[1] http://changingminds.org/explanations/stress/stress_costs.htm

of these conditions, which often lead to stress and a feeling of being out of control.

But you're not powerless. One strategy for reducing stress in these environments is to think about what is in your control, what you can influence, and what is out of your control that you may need to let go of.

First, begin with thinking about what is within your control, which is primarily an inside job—meaning that something external happens, which you then react to. But in most cases, you have control over your reactions. You can choose to get angry, frustrated, or anxious. Or, you can choose to take a few deep breaths and think about what a positive way would be for you to respond to the situation and focus on that. Is that difficult? Yes. But impossible? No. Authors such as Viktor Frankel and Elie Wiesel, who were concentration camp survivors, detailed how important their attitude was when it came to surviving such a brutal and inhumane ordeal.

How we choose to interpret situations and how we feel about them is largely within our control, as are the actions we can take in response. However, an even larger category exists, which includes things that we may not be able to fully control, but can influence. Influencing skills are one of the hottest subjects in leadership development today, in large part due to matrixed environments where leaders have to get work done through others despite not having position power to do so. In these cases, the leader's ability to influence through personal power, trying to understand and meet the other person's needs, and a willingness to compromise can be key.

The most effective leaders work to expand their circle of influence for the good of the organization, while ineffective leaders abdicate their responsibility to wield greater influence. The leaders who can influence effectively are often on fast tracks to even greater responsibility and influence.

Becoming Clear About What You Can Control or Influence

Much stress results from our worrying about things that are outside of our ability to influence or control. So-called "control freaks" behave the way they do in an attempt to minimize their stress by controlling people, places, and things. But the reality is that this rarely works, and even if it works in the short term, it can create frustration and resentment in those they are trying to control.

Maybe a better response is to get clear about things we can control and things we can influence, and apply our efforts in those directions. Even when we find ourselves worrying about things outside of both areas, we may be able to take positive action. For instance, we may worry about all the hungry people in our country. Maybe we could take the step of giving up one meal per week and donate the money saved to a local food bank or charity that supports the homeless or working poor. Rather than feeling overwhelmed by the magnitude of the problem, which can create chronic stress, take small actions that are within your control that contribute to effective solutions. As Eleanor Roosevelt once said, "It is better to light a candle than to curse the darkness."

Cultivating Humor and Perspective in Everyday Life

In today's VUCA world, it can be challenging to find humor in everyday life when we're working long hours, have responsibilities to family, and may volunteer to worthy causes. But some of the most effective and happy people I know, people with a lot on their plate, are always quick with a smile, self-deprecating joke, or laugh. They don't take themselves too seriously and seem to be grateful for life's challenges that come their way.

Humor is one of the qualities that partners bring to a successful marriage. More than good looks or shared interests, having a sense of humor and helping your spouse laugh is one of the keys to a long, happy marriage.

Appropriate humor can help to defuse a stressful situation. For example, some years ago, I was waved over by a police officer with a radar gun on the side of an interstate highway. As I sat in my car waiting for him to complete his paperwork, I silently fumed while watching all these other drivers speeding down the road even faster than I was.

When the officer approached my window to give me a ticket, I lost it. Now, normally if I get pulled over, I am very polite (not that I get pulled over a lot!), but this time, I was hot. I blurted out,

"Why are you giving me a ticket? What about all these other people going by who are speeding?" At this, the officer gave a slight chuckle and said, "Hey buddy, don't take it personally. You were the only one who pulled over!" In an instant, my mood lightened as I couldn't help but laugh at his comment. I went from having a really bad experience to having an experience that I could learn from and put into perspective. By the way, I haven't gotten pulled over for speeding since!

Laugh for the Health of It

It has been shown that laughter has a multitude of tangible health benefits, including lower blood pressure, a reduction in stress hormone levels, and a release of endorphins. When we were children, we laughed easily and frequently, but as we grew into adulthood, not so much. In fact, according to *Psychology Today*, the average four-year-old laughs 300 times per day. The average forty-year-old? Only four. [2]

> *"All grown-ups were once children... but only few of them remember it."*
> — Antoine de Saint-Exupéry, *The Little Prince*

Norman Cousins famously documented the positive effects of laughter with regards to the reduction of chronic pain he was suffering from—ten minutes of hearty laughter would bring him two hours of pain-free sleep. So, the health benefits that come from humor and laughter are tangible and significant.

But here's the thing I found most startling: That the human body cannot perceive the difference between a fake laugh and a real one! That forcing yourself to laugh is just as healthful as spontaneous laughter is.

As a result, there is now a practice called Laughing Yoga, as well as Laughing Clubs, which originated in India but have sprung up around the world. In these sessions, people are instructed to force

---

[2]   https://www.psychologytoday.com/us/blog/the-possibility-paradigm/201106/youre-not-laughing-enough-and-thats-no-joke

themselves to laugh for a period of time, which allows them to reap the rewards that laughter brings.

But in my own simple experiments, I've found that fake laughter transforms into real laughter very quickly. For instance, during a speech, I will occasionally instruct the audience to make eye contact with someone nearby and just start laughing and to keep doing so for twenty seconds. When I say "Go!" things start slowly but build rapidly, to the point where the entire room is in a genuine uproar. The first time I tried this to a room of 500 people, it took me a full five minutes to get them to stop laughing and to regain control!

So, whether you laugh in the shower, in the car, or decide to read or watch things that make you laugh, make a commitment to laugh more and watch your stress levels drop.

Practicing Mindfulness

Another tool for becoming more centered is to develop the practice of mindfulness. In its most simplistic form, mindfulness is about noticing what you're thinking about, as well as paying attention to the here and now.

So many of us go through life without being fully present. What I mean is that we often fall into the trap of regretting the past, or thinking and worrying about the future to the point where we're missing the only moment we are guaranteed to have—the *now*.

The best leaders I've worked with have the uncanny ability to put aside the past and the future and simply be present in the now. I observed this several years ago with a Global Sales Leader for a multinational company. I was leading a leadership retreat, and we invited him to join us for dinner that evening.

At the time, there were a lot of things going on in the business, including a recent acquisition, new go-to-market strategies, and external competitive pressures. But when he came to be with us, none of those stresses came through. In fact, when he spoke to individuals during the cocktail hour, it was amazing to observe just how present he really was. He made eye contact with everyone, didn't look at his phone once, remembered children's names, and listened attentively. I made a point of privately complimenting him on this behavior, and he told me that it didn't come naturally, but that he worked hard at being fully present so he could be with people in the moment. This leader, despite having high expectations and driving his teams hard, was much beloved by his people. I now understood one of the reasons why.

I had my own epiphany in this area some years ago, when I took my family on a hike in Sedona, Arizona. We were on the last day of a weekend trip and wanted to hike a beautiful area called Boynton Canyon. I mapped out the trail, calculated how long it would take for a round trip, and decided that if we hurried, we could squeeze it in before we needed to head back to Phoenix.

The entire hike out to the headwall of the canyon, I was obsessed with time. I kept looking at my watch and urging my family to pick up the pace. "Come on, we're almost there!" Whenever my son wanted to stop to look at a flower or grove of trees, I said, "We don't have time for that now. Let's go."

Finally, we reached the headwall of the canyon and paused for several minutes to take in the vista and snap a few photos. Then the drill sergeant (me) got everyone moving again back down the trail to the car. About five minutes after leaving the headwall, we passed a couple heading in the opposite direction. The man, clearly out of breath, asked me, "How much longer to the top?" I replied, "Not too much longer, but don't worry, the view is worth the hike." His female companion on his heels heard what I said, and as she passed, said, "The hike is worth the hike."

I was stopped dead in my tracks as if struck by lightning. *The hike is worth the hike!* At that moment, I realized how much we had missed on the hike due to my needing to get to the destination.

From that point forward, I slowed down and noticed things I had completely missed on the inbound hike. Beautiful flowers, chirping birds, red rocks, and the smell of the forest. Since that experience, I always try to remember that the hike is worth the hike or, if you will, the moment is worth the moment. Give it the attention it deserves.

Changing Repetitive Thoughts

Mindfulness isn't just about being present in our lives, but it also applies to noticing what we're thinking about. Why is this an important tool in living a centered life? It is because frequently, just below the level of consciousness, our thoughts are creating distraction and stress. In a 2005 article, the *National Science Foundation* suggested that we have between 12,000 and 60,000 thoughts per day and that 95% of them are repetitive (the same thoughts we had yesterday), and 80% of them are negative.[3] No wonder so many of us are walking stress balls!

Fortunately, mindfulness is a hot topic today. There is a multitude of books written on the subject and how to practice it, and some organizations I work with even offer mindfulness training to their employees.

As mentioned previously, our reactions to stimuli and our thoughts are largely within our control. A first step in changing those thoughts is to become aware of what they are. Once we become aware of our negative or repetitive thoughts, we can create affirmations that can serve to counter those thoughts and create a mindset shift.

For example, if we sit quietly for five minutes a day and notice that we are worried about job security, we can counter that negative thought by affirming something like, "I can only control the quality of the work I produce. I will let go of losing my job because that is out of my control."

You don't have to be part of a monastic order or a guru on a mountaintop to practice mindfulness and to be in the present moment. Small adjustments in these areas can create significant breakthroughs and help us lead a more centered life.

High Impact Actions for Centeredness

Here are some actions you can take to bring greater balance and perspective to your life.

---

[3] https://www.exploringtheproblemspace.com/new-blog/2017/1/1/counting-thoughts-part-i

Control and influence: Take inventory

As mentioned earlier, taking stock of things that are within your control or influence can be an effective way to channel your energies appropriately and to avoid wasting thought time on things that are out of your control, thus reducing the stress in your life.

⇒ **HIGH IMPACT ACTION:** Using a notebook or computer, create a list of items that are within your control, a list of items that are within your ability to influence, and a list of items that are outside of both areas. Once completed, ask yourself the following questions:

- Are there items within my circle of influence that I can actually control? What would be the benefit of doing so?
- Are there items outside of both areas (circle of concern) that I can actually have a degree of influence over? Are there items I need to practice letting go of?

Revisit the list regularly and become more aware during your day as to where situations should be placed for maximum effect.

Being fully present in the now

How mindful are you as you go about your day? When you engage with others, are you distracted, thinking about the next thing to say, or worrying about some issue you're dealing with? People can tell when you're not fully present, and you may miss an opportunity to strengthen a relationship or learn something new.

⇒ **HIGH IMPACT ACTION:** Make a decision to give your undivided attention to someone today at work or home. Really listen to what they are saying and practice active listening techniques: Eye contact, nodding, restating what they just said. Reflect on the experience afterward to see how that was different for you, and what insights you gained from being fully present. Keep a journal of your thoughts, and make an effort to do this more often every day.

Laughter is the best medicine

Do you laugh more like a four-year-old (300 times per day) or like a forty-year-old (four times per day)? The physical and mental health benefits of real or fake laughter are well documented, so get laughing!

⇒ **HIGH IMPACT ACTION:** Choose a time each day where you can force yourself to laugh heartily for three minutes. Maybe when you're in the shower first thing in the morning, or in the car on the way to work, or as you get a run or bike ride in. Or if you have a receptive partner, have them join in the fun with you (remember, making eye contact with someone else who's laughing will quickly transform pretend laughter into the real deal). Do this every day for a week and take note of how you feel. Do you feel less stressed? Are you less short and more patient with others? Are you sleeping better? Small actions can reap huge results, so keep it up and look for other ways to incorporate laughter into your life!

Take the Stress Quiz

Take the following quiz to better understand how much stress is negatively impacting your life. Be honest in your responses! The scoring grid follows.

Stress Quiz

Instructions: For each question, fill in the number that best describes you, and then add to total your score.

5 = All the time 4 = Most of the time 3 = Sometimes 2 = Rarely 1 = Never

Do you:

☐ Eat poorly?

☐ Try to do everything yourself?

☐ Blow up easily?

☐ Have unrealistic goals?

☐ Fail to see the humor in situations others find funny?

☐ Lose patience quickly with loved ones?

☐ Make a big deal of everything?

☐ Feel overwhelmed?

☐ Have difficulty making decisions?

☐ Feel out of control and disorganized?

☐ Use food or alcohol to cope with life?

☐ Keep everything inside?

☐ Neglect exercise?

☐ Have few close friends?

☐ Have difficulty sleeping?

☐ Feel sad or weepy?

☐ Put things off until later?

☐ Think there is only one right way to do something?

☐ Fail to build relaxation and reflection time into your day?

☐ Feel like God is far away?

☐ Worry a lot about the economy?

☐ Spend time complaining about the past or what could have been?

☐ During the past month, have you been bothered by any illness or fears about your health?

☐ During the past month, have you been feeling tired, worn out, used up, or exhausted?

TOTAL SCORE _____

How did you score?

Score	Rating	Analysis
Less than 48	Excellent	Your stress is well managed and doesn't impact your health or attitude
49–65	Good	For the most part, you manage your stress and don't let it impact your health or attitude
66–82	Fair	There are clear areas that you need to work on to reduce stress-related impacts in your life
83–99	Poor	Stress is a major challenge for you, and you need to take significant steps to combat it
100+	Danger Zone	You are under severe stress and need to take immediate action to prevent further damage to your physical and emotional health

The One Thing to Remember Even if You Forget Everything Else in This Chapter: CHRONIC STRESS WILL TAKE YOU DOWN!

Centeredness isn't a nice to do, it's a *need to do*. Don't let chronic stress undermine your emotional, physical, and spiritual health. If actions such as getting enough rest, eating well, and exercise don't help reduce your stress and become a more centered person, get the help you need to make the necessary changes in your life.

CHAPTER 7

The Seventh C: Commitment
Making a decision and staying on course

My wife Jody and I met at a conference in Orlando back in the late '80s, at a time when she was living in Denver and I was in Boston. We immediately hit it off, spending a great deal of time together during that week, and exchanged contact info at the end of the conference.

Over the following six months, we kept in touch, with occasional phone calls and letters. Early the next year, she accepted an invitation to fly to Boston for my annual Saint Patrick's Day party, and our friendship blossomed into a true romance.

For the next year, we flew back and forth to visit each other, then, fortunately, she had an opportunity to transfer to Boston for work. Three months later, I bought a one-way ticket to Denver, we loaded up her U-Haul and made the cross-country drive to Boston. She got her own apartment and for the next year or so grew closer together as we spent more time together.

For these reasons, Jody was ready to take the next big step in our relationship—to get engaged to be married. I, on the other hand, was taking it a bit more slowly. If you've heard of a "crawl, walk, run" strategy, mine was more like a "crawl, crawl, then crawl some more" strategy. You see, I had been burned in a previous relationship and was in no hurry to make a bigger commitment. Also, while the relationship was going great, it wasn't what I would call "perfect," and I kept waiting for "perfect" to show up before I felt comfortable making a lifelong commitment.

Well, my approach was wearing thin on Jody, so I felt I had to make a bold move to keep her from bolting. So, when one of my three roommates moved out, I thought it would be a great idea to have Jody move in. Jody and three male roommates. What was wrong with that? (This only goes to show how clueless I was.)

When I excitedly proposed this arrangement to Jody, I did not receive the response I was hoping for. Rather, she said something along the lines of something having to freeze over before that would happen. Confused, I went home to think about things.

Two days later, I went to her apartment for dinner. Her dad loved to go fishing and would always send her frozen fillets, so tonight we were cooking fish in the oven along with several side dishes.

I had no inkling of what I was about to ask her. You see, anyone who knows me knows that I'm a big-time planner, and if I had planned to ask her to marry me that evening, it would have been a show, trust me—balloons, marching band, maybe even a ring! But believe me, I had no such plans.

However, as I was taking the baked fish out of the oven, I found myself saying words that I couldn't believe were coming out of my mouth. I mean, I was literally having an out-of-body experience, which leads me to believe that a higher power knew what was better for me than I did and decided this one needed some direct assistance.

So, not so romantically, I said to Jody, "So, do you want to get married or what?" Jody, to her credit, knew an opportunity when presented with one, and quickly said yes. We hugged and cried as the fish got cold.

Now, here's the amazing lesson from my perspective. I had been waiting for the relationship to be perfect before popping the question, but I had it completely backward. For what I immediately discovered was by making the lifelong commitment, the relationship was perfect. Thirty-plus years later and we've never looked back. Our commitment to each other has never wavered.

The Power of Commitment

Making and keeping commitments, whether it be to ourselves, others, or our organizations, is what separates people who are practically inspired from those who merely "check the boxes." Without true commitment, it is all too easy to get discouraged, give up, or rationalize that the effort was misdirected or "wasn't worth it."

How many people had dreams they ached to fulfill when younger but didn't have the true commitment to see them to fruition? When I had my epiphany to become a speaker and writer at the age of forty, I knew I had to make some brave moves to support that commitment. Within three months of making that decision, we had moved from Boston to Arizona (without knowing a soul), and I embarked on a new career and had left all I had known behind.

Part of our rationale for moving to Arizona was business-related. Arizona was a major conference and meeting destination area, meaning I would find more speaking opportunities here than other places, as well as having a great airport for when I had to travel. Part of the rationale was for personal reasons, as my Texan wife had had enough of New England winters and longed to move to a warmer climate (boy, did we achieve that goal!). However, perhaps the most important part of my rationale in making such a radical move was to ensure that I would remain steadfast to my dream and not waver in my commitment.

One other way I solidified my commitment happened before we left Boston. A month before we were scheduled to leave, Jody threw me a birthday party, and many of our family and friends were in attendance. At one point during the celebration, I asked for everyone's attention and broke the news regarding our decision to move to Arizona and my new career. People were shocked but very supportive, and I felt grateful for each and every one of them.

But when the party was over and all the guests had left, I looked at Jody and said, "Well, I guess we really have to do this now!" By making a public commitment, I had made myself accountable for following through and doing what I said I would. Like the old military adage says, sometimes, in order to take the island, you have to burn the boats.

At its essence, commitment says that you believe in and value yourself, and are willing to take whatever steps are necessary, whatever sacrifices are needed, to create the inspired life of your dreams.

Commitment is also key to a lasting, loving relationship. Some years ago, my wife and I attended a marriage workshop. When we walked through the door, there was a banner hung high over the dais. It read *Love is a Decision*. At first, I wasn't sure what that meant, but then it was explained to us. There are times in a relationship when love is a feeling or emotion, especially when the relationship is new, and the honeymoon period is in full swing. But then there are times when for whatever reason—maybe your partner hurt you in some way or let you down—that love needs to become a decision. A decision—or commitment—to take the right action, to do the right thing, to remain committed to making things work out. If both partners are committed to the relationship, there is almost no hurdle that cannot be overcome.

> *"Whatever you can do or dream you can, begin it.*
> *Boldness has genius, power and magic in it!"*
> — W. H. Murray

Let's Say It Once More—Being Committed to Continuous Learning Is Key

In today's VUCA world, being committed is an ongoing and never-ending process of learning. It is the key to lasting success and fulfillment. Entire industries are created and destroyed in months, and positions that existed five or even two years ago may now be obsolete or have at least evolved into something that looks completely different with distinct skill sets required. Rather than becoming discouraged by this, reframe it as an opportunity for continuous growth and expansion, and learn to take matters into your own hands. Seek out opportunities to learn new skills, read blogs, articles, or books that challenge your current worldview and promote deep reflection and new perspectives. Become comfortable with being uncomfortable. Quoted earlier in this book, educator Eric Hoffer stated that the learners would inherit the earth.

Learning takes many forms and doesn't only include formal education or training. Part of practicing mindfulness, which I discussed in the previous chapter, involves paying attention to the world around you. The more you pay attention, the more you learn from the people around you, trends that are happening, and where your strengths and weaknesses are.

Once you've learned a new skill or approach, the key is to anchor it in so that it becomes part of who you are and how you work. Research into training programs indicates that if all someone does is attend a training class, only 12–15% of what they learned gets applied to the job.[1] There are several ways to combat this abysmal adoption rate. For starters, creating a practical action plan, which includes what you will do, when you will do it, and what impacts you will achieve by doing it, will help you to be accountable. Even top performers benefit from having written goals, so get clear and specific in these areas. Written goals can include short-term actions as well as long-term goals, and using SMART[2] criteria to develop the goals is another tip for ensuring accountability and measurable impact.

Sharing those goals with a significant other, mentor, or your manager takes the accountability one step further. Keeping them front and center so that you see or revisit them regularly is important, too. Whenever a good friend of mine sets a goal for himself, he posts it on his bathroom mirror so that it's the first thing he sees every morning, and it's the last thing he sees at night.

Find whatever tricks work for you, in order to sustain and extend your learnings. You're never too young or too old to begin this practice. Late in his life, when he was well into his eighties, the great Renaissance artist Michelangelo is reported to have written on one of his sketches, *Ancora imparo*. Translated, it means, "I am still learning."

Getting a Little Better Every Day

One trait that I've noticed among high performing, inspired people, is that they never settle for the status quo, but seek to improve every day, even if only by a little bit. People who are dedicated to physical fitness and working out practice this regularly. Can I run this 10K a little faster than last week? Can I lift a little more weight today than I did a few days ago? Can I shave a few seconds off my half-mile swim? Setting incremental improvement goals helps to motivate and inspire greater performance and is a fun way to remain committed to a program of exercise.

I, too, think about this often. Am I getting better or worse? What am I doing to improve, even just a little bit today? What small but consistent habits can I embrace on a regular basis to expand my

---

[1]   Dr. Robert Brinkerhoff, *High Impact Learning*
[2]   SMART = Specific, Measurable, Actionable, Realistic and Time bound

capability over time? Incremental improvements, made consistently over time, lead to improved performance and real breakthroughs.

Dealing with Procrastination

Despite our best intentions and efforts, there are times when we put off doing things that we know we should be doing. If this happens occasionally, be gentle with yourself by remembering that you are only human and that all of us have off-days occasionally. However, if you find this becoming a pattern, or find that a day of procrastination turns into weeks or months, then you need to take immediate action to right the ship and get back on the path to an inspired life.

One of the reasons I've seen people procrastinate or even give up on their goals is perfectionism, a need to either do things perfectly or not at all. Well, sorry to be the bearer of bad news, but being imperfectly human is part of our condition! While holding "perfect" up as an ideal to strive towards, recognize that progress, not perfection, should be the mindset. The path toward mastery is never a straight line; we are bound to encounter setbacks or plateaus along the way.

The key is to not get discouraged, but to keep putting in the effort, keep taking the next right action. If you find yourself mentally discouraged, action is the best medicine. Often, we can't think our way out of a negative mindset, but we can act our way out of it. Get into action and watch your mood change for the better.

Other steps for avoiding procrastination include creating a checklist for each day, starting with the most challenging or difficult action first, not overcommitting yourself (which leads to overwhelm), and building in little rewards for small accomplishments. Being good to yourself builds greater self-esteem and respect, which helps to maintain your commitment to yourself during times of challenge or struggle.

High Impact Actions for Commitment

Here are some actions you can take to support and reinforce your commitment to living a practically inspired life.

What's in the way?

Do you find yourself setting goals or committing to actions but are having difficulty following through? Then apply the courage needed to uncover what is in the way and how you can minimize or mitigate those real or perceived obstacles.

⇒ **HIGH IMPACT ACTION:** Brainstorm a list of things that interfere with your willingness or ability to consistently commit to a plan of action and personal development. These obstacles may include external commitments, people, or internal self-talk that is limiting you. Conduct this exercise in a spirit of self-perception, not self-deception. When you've exhausted the list, put it aside for a while then come back to it again to see if you've missed anything.

Once your list is created, narrow it down to the top two or three obstacles that are getting in the way.

For each one of these obstacles, think about what actions you can take or beliefs you can shift to minimize or eliminate the obstacle. Then, write down the positive benefits you will receive by successfully overcoming each hurdle.

My Top Obstacles to Progress	How Can I Minimize or Eliminate this?

Extra Credit: Share your work with your mentor or accountability buddy and ask them to check in with you regularly to gauge your progress.

Create a point system

Make your plan of action to create an inspired life a game that you can keep score with. When I was in a new sales role, my manager had us implement a point system that helped us focus on the activities that would lead to success. For example, meeting someone new and exchanging contact information would be worth one point, a new prospect meeting was worth five points, a proposal would be worth ten points, etc. There were a number of other sales-related activities that also had points associated with them. The goal was to achieve a minimum of 100 points per week. The motivating factor here was that even if sales weren't flying in the door, I was reassured that by hitting my point total every week, I was doing the things that, over time, would lead to lasting success.

⇒ **HIGH IMPACT ACTION:** Identify the key actions you've committed to that need attention every week. Rank these actions in order of importance, then assign a relative point value to each. For example, if there are items labeled one to ten from most important to less important, assign a point value of ten to item number one, a point value of nine to item number two, etc. Create a table or spreadsheet to log your progress, and refer to it every morning and at the end of each day to check your progress and plan the next day's activities.

The One Thing to Remember Even If You Forget Everything Else in This Chapter: STICK WITH THE WINNERS!

Identify people in your life who are living practically inspired lives and study their habits. What creates their success and inspiration? I guarantee it's not due to dumb luck or accident. Surround yourself with people who inspire you to be better tomorrow than you are today!

CHAPTER 8

Living Under Full Sail
The fruits of an inspired life

Our lives are made up of days, and our days are made up of moments. Nobel Prize author and researcher Daniel Kahneman once posited that we have over 20,000 moments in each day.[1] Some of those moments grab our attention, such as a meeting with an important client or having lunch with an old friend, while others slip by barely unnoticed.

I once heard a story about an executive that was working with a coach, and the coach was waiting in the lobby of the executive's office to meet with him for their weekly session. Suddenly the executive practically ran in the door, laptop in arms, wild-eyed and breathless. "I'll be with you in a minute," he said while he turned the corner to his office.

The coach followed him in hot pursuit as the exec made his way past rows of offices and cubicles, keeping up a full head of steam and head down in a brisk walk. When he arrived at his office, he flipped open his laptop, and while it was rebooting, the coach walked in the door. "I'll just be a couple of minutes," said the executive. "I have some important work to attend to."

The coach stopped him in his tracks. "You see that row of offices and cubicles full of people in them that you just stormed by? *There's* your work."

How many moments do we miss every day because we're distracted or disengaged? Many leaders I work with privately complain

---

1   https://www.fit4market.com/20-000-moments-a-day

of being overwhelmed with the sheer volume of items they must deal with every day. Many express frustrations at having to deal with problems all the time versus the fun part of leading people, such as creating a vision, strategies to achieve it, and developing the people to successfully execute on it.

When I hear those sentiments, I express my empathy but also make it clear that while we don't always have choices about what we have to do, we have total control over how we do it or react to it. Yes, this takes some practice and discipline. Still, people who have mastered this can stay positive and centered amid life and work challenges, see the glass as half full versus half empty, and are able to keep focused on their values and goals despite occasional setbacks.

That, to me, is what it means to be practically inspired.

Practically inspired people are like the modern-day lamplighters of old. Before the advent of electric lights, each night, lamplighters took to the streets to ignite the streetlamps that illuminated the night. Without the lamplighters, there would be no light, only darkness. By lighting the way, they allowed others to find their own paths, journey safely and securely, and do things they otherwise wouldn't have been able to do.

People living lives of practical inspiration not only create more fulfilling and successful lives for themselves but through direct contact with others, and the power of their example inspires others to achieve more, to be more. They are a blessing to all.

Enjoying Each Day

Practically inspired people are the epitome of the Latin phrase "Carpe Diem." Seize the day! Despite the storms and struggles they encounter, they absolutely insist on making the best of every day, including mentally and emotionally. For some, this happens naturally; for others, it takes some practice.

"How are you today?" How many times in your life has someone asked you that question, usually as a form of greeting? How many times have you responded almost automatically, "Fine, how are you?" when in reality, you're not doing that great? Or, more precisely, your perception is that you aren't so great.

In my lifetime of experiences, it is rare for me to meet people who truly feel that they are doing great when appearances may be to the contrary. It's relatively simple to feel great when everything is lining up for you, when there's little mental angst from issues or conflicts with others or when circumstances aren't to your liking.

A wise old friend of mine would often greet people in the manner I described above, and if the answer came back, "I'm doing great," then he would usually respond with, "Well then, you must be getting your own way!"

Do you have to be "getting your own way" to feel like you're having a great day? What might it take to be able to genuinely feel like you're having a great day even when the stars aren't aligned in your favor?

Inspired people who have the ability to be happy regardless of external circumstances have several things in common. First, they are steadfast optimists (which, by the way, can be a learned trait). They perpetually look for the good in something that others might perceive as bad, and they trust that they'll be okay no matter what. Their mental self-talk is positive, and they don't allow themselves to dwell on negativity.

Second, they feel genuine gratitude for what they have in their life, instead of focusing on what they lack. As the saying goes, the happiest people want what they already have, instead of pining for what they don't have. Is there anything sadder than someone who wastes their life chasing after the next thing they think will bring them happiness—jobs, material possessions, relationships—only to discover (again) that the satisfaction they thought it would bring them isn't real or lasting?

Lastly, they find ways to be of service to others they come into contact with each day. In some instances, service may be a true helping hand to someone in need, like a stranger stuck on the side of the road with a flat tire. Or it could be as simple as offering a smile and a kind word to the cashier at the supermarket, the grouchy neighbor, or the homeless person on the street corner.

Life is too short to spend time in worry, anxiety, or other negative distractions that drain focus and vitality from the current moment. Sadly, some people wear "busy" like a badge of honor, and some organizations actually encourage it. But it doesn't have to be that way. Be attuned to ways to practice optimism, gratitude, and service in all the moments of your life so that when you are asked the question, "How are you doing today?" you can honestly and enthusiastically respond with, "I'm doing great!"

Some days, we have to look hard for the positive. One helpful trick is to be grateful for the things in our lives we often take for granted. If you have a place to live, enough food to eat, and people who care about you in your life, are you grateful for that? There are plenty of people who aren't so lucky.

Big Goals Require Small Actions

The advent of a new year is a time when many of us make resolutions to do things differently during the coming year. (Maybe buying this book and deciding to read it was one of your resolutions. If so, congratulations for making it this far!) However, for many people, some of those resolutions or goals have already dropped off the radar (February or March is a great time to buy slightly used exercise equipment on the cheap), while still others have fallen victim to the "I'll get to it tomorrow" rationalization. When we procrastinate or abandon new behaviors, we sabotage our efforts at self-improvement and growth as well as reinforce a negative cycle that is difficult to climb out of.

This can happen even when the goal is critical to our success or wellbeing, a "need to do" versus just a "nice to do." Life gets busy, passion turns to apathy, and before we know it, we've dropped the goal completely.

One way to break this vicious cycle is to break your goal into manageable chunks that you look at frequently, which this book has attempted to do. For example, when my wife sets a goal for herself, she writes it on a Post-it and slaps it on the bathroom mirror, so that it's the first thing she sees every morning and the last thing she sees at night. Research has found that even top performers benefit from having documented goals. Why? Because it fosters accountability and keeps the goals at the top of the mind. It's easier to keep your ship on course if you frequently take note of what the destination is!

For me, when I get stuck on the road to goal achievement, I ask myself, "What are three things I can do today to move toward my goal?" If it's a perceived obstacle that is stopping me, I think of actions I can take to minimize or mitigate the obstacle.

Taking these actions in one day won't necessarily get you to your goal or remove your obstacle completely, but they will get your energy flowing constructively again. They will also produce a greater sense of control and the personal power required to press on toward your goals.

Here's a sampling of some other small actions that can lead to big results:

- Remember, it's the little things done consistently that lead to lasting success. Want to read more this year, but can't find the time? Well, can you find ten minutes? If you can read for just ten minutes per day this year and you're an average reader, you should finish around six books this year.

- Want to sell more? Make just one extra sales call per day, and you'll talk to approximately 220 more people this year.

- How about friendships? Write one short note per day to a new acquaintance, long lost buddy, or dear companion. A friend of mine keeps a stack of blank note cards with stamps affixed nearby to make the process easier. He says, "These days, note cards stand out. They take more time and show more effort than just texting or sending an email."

Robin Sharma wrote, "The smallest of actions is greater than the noblest of intentions." Become a practically inspired person of focused, consistent action, and watch your impact, influence, and satisfaction soar.

In Closing

I would welcome any and all comments, success stories, or whatever you have to share regarding this book and how it has served you. My goal in writing it was not to create the next bestseller (although that would be nice) but to do two things. First, to capture in one place what I've learned and experienced in over thirty years of helping leaders and others reach their full potential. It's a topic that I feel passionate about and which practically inspires me, and I felt compelled to share it with others. It's trite but true: If only one person benefits from what is written here, then my labors have not been in vain.

Second, I wanted to leave a legacy for my family and friends that captured who I was and what I believed in. Maybe someday, my son will have his own family, and my grandkids will have a chance to know more about their grandpa and what he stood for.

If nothing else, writing this book has been simmering in my mind for a good twenty years now. Interestingly and fittingly, my own procrastination and fits of starts and stops were solved in large part by adopting the same tips and techniques that are espoused in this book. Therefore, you can feel comfortable that I've eaten my own cooking here, and I can wholeheartedly affirm that these approaches can serve you well.

Having said that, I'd like to add that not one of the ideas or approaches in this book will work for you. You heard me right; they just won't work for you. YOU HAVE TO WORK THEM. Just reading the book won't change a thing, it's taking the actions that will produce your desired results. Don't be like the frog on the log that just sits there. Take the leap, and great things are sure to follow.

Paul Schnabel speaks and offers workshops on the topics contained in this book. If you would like more information or wish to correspond on any related topic, contact information is below.

Contact Information:

Email: ptschnabel@gmail.com

Made in the USA
Coppell, TX
21 August 2020

34285547R00061